CW00852927

Tramps 47

from Prison
to Parkbench
to Pulpit

Lynette Sloane

authorHOUSE®

AuthorHouse™ UK Ltd.
500 Avebury Boulevard
Central Milton Keynes, MK9 2BE
www.authorhouse.co.uk
Phone: 08001974150

First published by AuthorHouse 2/23/2010

ISBN: 978-1-4490-6293-4 (sc)

This book is printed on acid-free paper.

Contents

Tramps – From Prison to Park Bench to Pulpit - Synopsis by Steve Sloane

This, the biography of Pastor Les Deane begins with the overview of his 1950s childhood in rural Lancashire. Les' parents were poor but his father was a hard worker and provided well for the 11 children, who had to sleep 4 to 5 in a bed. It tells of a family bound together with love until one day they are split apart due to the continual struggle by their father to stay in gainful employment.

These early years deeply contrast the next twenty or so years of his life. He becomes a member of one of the most ruthless gangs of 1960's London, and as a consequence, of his dealings he spends time in various prisons and remand centres where he receives vicious beatings from numerous prison officers.

Soon after his release from Norwich Prison, whilst totally disillusioned by all he has experienced, he drops out of society to become a tramp. The next five years are spent living on the streets, each day a struggle to survive. At times, he trudges the streets, having not eaten for a week, existing in the soaking wet and biting cold. He becomes an alcoholic—this is the only way to block out the cold on the long winter nights. Summer months produce easier times, and sometimes even humour can be found—such as, when joined by two other tramps, they unsuccessfully tried to catch a duck in an old blanket, with the consequence of all three of them ending up in a pond.

This part of the story shows the dignity and humanity of street-people, who were someone's baby, warm and loved. Now they are homeless, treated with contempt and even rejected by parts of the Church.

After five years on the streets, his health is failing and only later does he realise how near to death he is. He is finally taken in by a family whose love and care help him become a reformed character, eventually finding his faith in God and becoming a Church Minister.

Today, he is Pastor and Manager of Freshfields Christian Music Ministries, a Christian music group which ministers at various Churches throughout the country.

Having preached at more than 200 different churches over a five year period he has been asked on numerous occasions to write his biography.

Tramps 47 is his story.

Introduction

The purpose of this book is to bear witness that for the lost and despairing, there is hope; there is a Saviour, Jesus Christ, and a God who really cares. By relating my experiences I hope to show that the chains of life can be broken. I've been as truthful as possible in describing all the experiences I encountered in my search for what had been missing from my life, only changing some names and locations to respect others peoples anonymity.

For so many years I'd been wearing blinkers that blinded me to the truth. God so loved me that he removed my blindness, and broke every chain that bound me. He brought me to the foot of the cross and showed me his great love. By repenting of my sins, and accepting for myself what Jesus Christ did for me on that cross, I'm now cleansed of every sin and wrong doing, and am experiencing fulfilment in God's love for me daily. Through His Holy Spirit God has given me new life and a testimony of his saving grace, and has shown me his undeserved love and favour.

Formerly ensnared in the world of crime and violence, and later confined behind bars, I experienced fear and hate; my mind was bent on despair with nowhere to turn, then soon after regaining my freedom I dropped out of society to become a tramp.

The romance of crime was destroyed; life became pitiful. My body, my bones were so cold; any hope I once held in life was cruelly destroyed. I felt loneliness, hunger, and thirst. I felt pain reaching down to the depths of my being, but then a message arrived—a message of deliverance, warmth, love, and care—and yes, it was true.

I heard the Gospel and responded. God does care.

May God bless you, and all the people who loved and cared for me through the hard times. - Thank you for your prayers.

1.

Childhood Days

My story begins at 7.45 one Monday morning. It was early December 1955 and I was seven years old. Mother walked into the bedroom. "Okay", she shouted, "time for school".

My family consisted of Mum, Dad and eleven children. Taken from oldest to youngest I was number six. We all lived in a three bed-roomed council house, sleeping four or five children to a bed. I struck lucky with my bed as Dad put his old army coat on it to keep us warm. Downstairs, mother already had the breakfast table laid out. We rushed down the stairs, a stampede of wild animals, and were soon tucking into porridge and toast, followed by the usual spoonful of malt.

Dad had left for work earlier; his first job this and every winters morning was to light a nice coal fire. He was at various times, a baker, a coal man or a dustman; Dad would turn his hands to all kinds of work. No one could ever accuse him of being lazy; he was always a hard worker and good provider for his larger than average family.

I loved these cold winter mornings. Christmas was nearly upon us, and through the window I could see the snow starting to fall. As I hurriedly threw on my coat, I was thinking about all the icy-cold slides I would soon be making on my way to school. These were tremendous childhood days that today hold such wonderful memories.

This Christmas was very special, as Mum and Dad gave me a Davy Crocket outfit with hat and sharpshooter gun. I was so happy walking down the main street that morning wearing my outfit, and singing "Davy Crocket, King of the Wild Frontier". There was such innocence in childhood back then, and such happiness in children's faces as they unwrapped their presents on Christmas day. It didn't matter what the gift was, and it was even more special when their Dad had made the toys himself. The value of the present wasn't important; it was the joy of receiving that counted.

At dinnertime we all sat around the dining table, the places neatly set out with the turkey in the middle. It all looked so scrumptious. As we held hands and sang 'We wish you a Merry Christmas', my mouth was already watering. I could hardly wait to start eating. What a lovely Christmas time that was. If only life could have stayed that way.

The 1950's were a great era for most and there were many families like us—poor, yet happy to be alive—but out of all the children in my family I seemed to be the difficult one, and I tasted Dad's belt regularly.

One day when I came home from school Mum and Dad gathered the family together, and told us that we were moving to another part of Britain. Our little worlds came crashing down.

We all chirped in, "What about our friends? What about Granny and Granddad? What about chasing the fire engine and the fields we play on?" We were troubled; our little worlds had come to an end. I couldn't believe it was happening and certainly didn't understand why. My older brothers were to stay with Grandma; our family was to be torn apart. Suddenly, we were to wave goodbye to the home we were born in.

Although Mum and Dad defended their decision to move, insisting that it was for the best, we were far from convinced.

"Who's it best for?" we asked.

We weren't looking forward to our move, but the dreaded day soon arrived, and we found ourselves in a village called Coppell, just outside Chorley in Lancashire. The street was named Bogburn Lane. What a name! However, it had gas lamps and farm fields all around it. To a child it promised such exciting times ahead, and yet there were also to be sad times. Life was always a mixture of such adventures.

Our house was a very old fashioned terrace, with a roaring coal fire in winter, a tin bath, and an outside toilet with no flush. The toilet consisted of a metal bin that the council emptied once a week. There was no toilet roll, instead we used pieces of newspaper that Mum cut up into squares and tied onto string.

Since moving Dad worked on the Leonard Fairclough building site.

"Hard work", he'd say as he came home from 'a hard days graft', tossing his coat aside, and collapsing onto a chair. Mum made him a drink of tea in his pint-sized mug while he kicked off his shoes. Soon we'd eat. Sausage and mash was our customary meal, very nice too.

Our school was about a mile away. Sometimes we travelled there by bus but at other times, when we didn't have the bus fare, we had to walk. Phew! When you were only seven years old that was a long old walk to school, and I hated school. I just couldn't cope with it. I found any excuse to play truant and run down to the nearby bridge. There I would stand feeling the vibration in my feet as the trains speeded underneath, and smoke bellowed up all around me.

When I got home Mum would say, "You smell of smoke again. Keep away from those trains". Of course, I ignored her. I loved trains. I loved the smoke, the rumble and the squeal of wheels; it was wonderful. I'll never forget that bridge. To most local kids it was special. Standing there, you could let your imagination run away. What dreams I had as a child, so many of them good. Times were so innocent then, and the farmers allowed all the children the run of the fields, the barns, the haymaking, and spud and pea picking.

In this rural area the snowy season was so picturesque. Even as a child, I found the scenes of fresh snow scattered all over the fields, trees and house tops so beautiful. This was truly a season of good will. I thank God now for those happy times and memories, but life is full of surprises. I didn't know what was going to shape me, or what contrasts lay ahead.

Nearby there was an enormous field where the fair would set up every May time. We children would eagerly watch and cheer as it arrived.

"Hooray!" we would all shout. Now was the time for good behaviour, and collecting milk and pop bottles to get some pocket money. The shopkeepers gave us one old penny for a milk bottle and three old pennies for a pop bottle. I soon had lots of loose change for my rides. The fairground was every child's dream: the swings, roundabouts, waltzers, bumping cars, bright lights, candy floss, and toffee apples. I was the fun kid—into everything—but fairgrounds were only around for a week and afterwards life soon came back down to earth again. It wasn't long before I was back at school once more.

As I mentioned, I hated school; I simply dreaded going there. I was always one of the smallest in my class, and was bullied unmercifully by the other children. I couldn't cope with the teachers either. I suppose it was the discipline that I hated. Consequently, I decided there was only one way out, I would play truant. I skipped school many times, and became very good at making excuses for being absent.

We had a 'truant man', whose whole aim in life seemed to be riding around the area on a pushbike, looking for children like me who took days off school. He was very good at his job, seemingly appearing out of nowhere, so it was very hard to dodge him. If you got caught he'd take you to school, and the punishment was three strokes of the cane, two hundred lines, and worse still he'd visit your parents and let them know about it. Wow, my father would take off his leather belt to me, and then I couldn't sit down for a while. Both my parents were of the 'old school', very strict and moral.

Time passed, and at nearly ten years old my younger brother, Russell, and I started a hobby collecting wild birds such as magpies, jackdaws and owls. We kept them all imprisoned in the outhouse. One day as Mum was walking past her outhouse she heard strange noises coming from inside it, so she opened the door to investigate.

"Ahhh" She shrieked as several birds escaped past her, rushing for their freedom, flapping wildly and squawking.

"Les where are you?" She screamed without any hesitation, "I know this is you again. Wait 'til your Father gets home!" I couldn't understand what all the fuss was about. The birds were our pets. I'd taken the magpie out of its nest two days before it was due to leave the nest and had reared it myself. It was really tame. It would fly down from the trees to greet me every day as I returned from school, then fly into the house, stand on the dinner table and my brothers and sisters would feed it tidbits at meal times. Dad had never really approved of this but eventually got used to the idea, although he still frowned upon it.

We children loved nature. My older sister Pam had a little kitten. One summer's night, around nine o'clock, she put it out in the back garden for a walk, but my owl swooped down and killed it. This caused me a lot of trouble too. Mum and Dad were furious and told me the birds had to go. I was broken hearted.

I became a problem child, my life's Pattern now beginning to take shape. For some reason I thought it clever to steal from my parents, especially when I got away with it. Eventually Dad caught me and tried to show me the error of my ways, but it never really sank in. I rebelled at anything now. My schoolteachers never seemed to have any time for me either, as I was forever arguing with them. The only lesson I enjoyed was sports. I excelled at football, running and high jump. At sports day I won everything going, but even then got into trouble because the teachers told me to give the other children a chance and I wouldn't. The others might have been good at written work, but this was one thing I was good at, so I was determined to do my absolute best.

My parents couldn't understand such a drastic change in my personality. My childhood had become very troubled, and I was constantly being punished at school and at home. Trouble became my middle name, and even my brothers and sisters couldn't understand me.

I started to steal money, bicycles or anything. By my thirteenth birthday I was involved with three other like minded lads. We called ourselves 'The Lever Gang' because of the way we 'acquired' things. We wore leather coats with silver and gold studs, jeans, and pointed shoes.

My mindset was this, *I get beatings at school and more beatings at home; no one thinks I'll ever come to anything or do any good in my life, so why not become just what's expected of me?* I still loved my parents and my brothers and sisters, but I made it very hard for them to love me. The police regularly visited the house to speak to me about stolen cycles, but it was all to no avail; I refused to change my ways. On one occasion, as a type of revenge, I stole a policeman's cycle and dumped it in a river. I was loosing control of how far I would go, although my misdeeds were at this time still comparatively minor.

2.

My Motorbike Era

One day, on my way back from 'bird nesting' over the fields, I walked past a house, and spotted a B.S.A. Bantam motorcycle parked in the yard. I was so taken with the bike that I knocked on the door and asked if it was for sale.

The owner smiled and replied, "You can have it for five pounds."

Disappointed, I walked away thinking, *wow, if only I'd five pounds*; this was more than a week's wage.

When I got home I told Dad all about it. He stared at me for a moment appearing bewildered.

Up to this time I'd never had a close relationship with my father. He terrified me. I noticed he was wearing the same leather belt with large buckle that he often used to discipline me.

Dad was an authoritarian figure. Approaching him instilled a greater fear into my being, than all those occasions when I stood outside the headmaster's office, as a small child, having transgressed at school. Despite this, Dad was a practical, hands on type of person. If anyone asked him a question they would get a straight forward answer. I found it hard to love him, and we never voiced our feelings to each other or said we loved one other. Despite this there were also good times, when on those long, cold winter evenings, the whole family sat huddled around a coal fire and I felt safe and protected.

As I stood there waiting for Dad's answer, my mind flashed back to a particular Christmas day when I was nine or ten year's old. The dinning table was laid with the turkey set in the middle. I, and all my brothers and sisters were sitting around the table, excited and chattering as we waited to start the feast set before us. Our mouths were watering, but we knew not to start our meal because Dad hadn't arrived home yet.

Suddenly the front door opened, and we all turned to see Dad walk in. The excited chatter stopped because we could see that he was in a very bad mood. He had been drinking and looked angry. We didn't know why. Perhaps he had lost a game of darts or dominoes. He never needed an excuse.

He walked forwards and stood near to the dinning table.

Mum asked, "Where've you been? We're waiting here for our Christmas dinner."

"I'll tell you where I've been" he retorted, picking up the turkey and hurling it into the back of the open fire. Then he grabbed hold of the table and turned it over. Food and plates crashed to the floor and the children scattered. Dad started smashing the house up.

That day I was filled with hate for him. Mum had been up since daybreak preparing that meal, and now returned to the kitchen to cook us all egg and chips. We children gathered in the living room and watched the turkey burning in the fireplace; our dreams of a happy Christmas were shattered.

Despite these memories I'd felt brave enough to tell Dad about the motorcycle. It was only for a few moments that I stood there in front of him waiting for his response, but it seemed an eternity. My resolve weakened. Should I run out or just stay and face the usual hiding?

To my surprise he answered, "Okay. Let's go see the bike". I was speechless. The bike didn't work, but Dad said that he'd buy it anyway, adding, "It won't take long to fix". He was right; Russell and I had it working in two days. For a while I felt good inside, and was happy because Dad had bought the bike for me.

My days of motorbikes had started and a new chapter in my life had begun. Exciting times lay ahead, or so I thought. I learnt to ride my motorbike very quickly. Although it wasn't a Norton 500cc, or a Triumph, in my books it was 'thee' bike to have.

Overnight, at almost fourteen years old, I became a Greaser, or Rocker, as they were otherwise known. In those days we had Mods and Rockers, and Cliff Richard was number one. Mods rode scooters, with lots of mirrors on them, while rockers wore leather jackets and jeans, and rode motorcycles. There was great rivalry between these two gangs.

Many other youths of my age were now motorbike crazy too. Velocette, James, B.S.A.'s and many more exciting bikes were coming onto the streets. They may be considered 'oldie' bikes nowadays, but we youngsters loved them and were learning fast. It didn't matter how many times you fell off your bike, you just got back on.

The Sixties were here.   A mixture of cars appeared, including the Bubble Car, what a classic, and respected by all of that day.

My attitude began to change—and not for the better—although at the time I didn't know this. I'd left school at fourteen thinking that I was grown up. What a shock I had. When you leave school everything suddenly becomes different. I went to the interview for my first job, at the local cotton mill in Coppell, feeling very nervous indeed. Suddenly I wasn't so grown up.

The foreman wanted to see my school records. My heart sank, because I knew they didn't look good, but I got the job anyway.

"Start Monday" he said. I walked home with my spirit lifted. Telling Mum and Dad made me feel better about myself at last. My wages were three pounds and ten shillings, which is the modern equivalent of three pounds fifty pence.

"Not bad", Dad said on hearing my news. Of course I would have to give up my paper round. That was sad; I enjoyed earning my ten shillings a week. In those days it was good money. Still, life goes on, now I was a worker earning a proper living. Somewhere God had his hand on my life, but like so many other surprises that lay ahead, I'd only find this out much later on in life.

For me, the sixties was a fantastic era. I felt I was, as that film says, 'A rebel without a cause'. The music was great and we were very fortunate to have Radio Luxemburg and Radio Caroline. Radio Caroline was a rebel music station that broadcasted from a ship. It was founded during March 1964, and gave us all the great music of the day until it was impounded in 1968, although it enjoyed various comebacks at later dates.

The Beatles had hit the scene, and I was one of their many thousands of fans. I actually saw them live in Wigan. What a concert that was: Gene Pitney, Roy Orbison and the Beatles all together on one night!

Flower power began to flourish. The Jesus People arrived, giving flowers to every passer by, and Rock and Roll was at its height. I was getting wilder, a fully-fledged Rocker with a chip on my shoulder. I loved working in the cotton mill though. The people were so friendly and I met my first love there. She was a pretty sixteen year old named Valerie. I'll always remember her long, blonde hair and lovely blue eyes. This was one of the few times I ever had feelings for another person, until much later on in life.

Work at the mill was hard but enjoyable, yet for some reason I always felt something was missing from my life, if only I'd known then what I know now. I was dissatisfied with life in general. Soon Valerie and I went our different ways. This was sad; your first love always holds a special place in your heart.

My parents were finding me increasingly difficult to understand. To fit in with everyone else around me I started drinking, smoking and gambling, which seemed the normal thing to do, but left me feeling empty inside. I was becoming very discontented and frustrated, and getting into fights in pubs and clubs. My bad reputation began to grow. There was police involvement too. My poor parents were going spare, and even my brothers and sisters were now keeping me at arms length.

I started going out with girls, but only used them. My life was getting worse and going down hill fast. Mum and Dad threw me out.

"Enough is enough" Dad said. That was sad too.

I quit my job. I had the '*I'm seventeen and no one can tell me what to do attitude.*' When you're in that condition friends leave you like the plague and no one can get through to you. I found a one roomed flat and signed on the dole. I was finding living hard, although jobs were plentiful. One week I went though three but couldn't settle down into any of them.

I met up with my gang. We all had one thing in common, chips on our shoulders and the notion that no one could bother us. These were the right ingredients for a big come down. We got into more fights; we started fights anywhere. Wigan was to become our territory and my downfall. I had a special hate for authority, especially the police, and they felt the same way about me. My life was sliding downhill.

3.

The Slippery Slope

The Lever Gang began to split. Two of my friends became scared of where I was heading, so they left and went on to lead good lives. Nowadays I'm happy they did as someone like me could have led them to jail. My other friend became a 'Born Again Christian', whatever that was. He'd met a group of Pentecostals talking about Jesus. Oh boy was I mad about that. I saw the change in my friend but couldn't grasp why it had happened. I only knew that it was good for him. Me? I was into my own world. As usual I started feeling sorry for myself. Although I didn't yet realise it, I was my own worst enemy.

It was a Saturday night, so I visited my local pub which was packed out. Cigarette smoke hung heavily in the air. We all sat there drinking, smoking and 'talking football' in the dingy bar. Gazing down at the table I noticed all the spilled beer and ashtrays overflowing with dog ends and ash, and thought to myself, *is this life? Never! I need lots of money to have the lifestyle I want and there is only one way to get it. Who says crime doesn't pay, we'll see about that!*

There is nothing worse than when you cannot see the obvious right in front of you, but for some reason I was blinded to reality. I'd cut friends and family out of my life without even realising it, so I felt lonely, unwanted, uncared for, and rejected. I just didn't know what life was about; I was so immature. I felt empty inside and had no idea how to fill that void.

At about one o'clock that morning I met up with a few friends.

They seemed as fed up as I did so I said, "Why don't we do a job, rob a Dance Hall?" They agreed.

In the centre of Wigan there was a place called 'The Room at the Top'. We decided it would be a good place to burgle. Using the metal drain pipe, we scaled the wall to the rooftop, removed some slates, and climbed down through the roof into the building.

The alarm was easy to disarm, even for amateurs, but we didn't realise there was a separate alarm for the front door. It was on a different circuit and we must have tripped it off, because whilst we were inside the bar robbing the cash register and fruit machines, I heard the door open at the bottom of the building.

I looked down and saw several police on the stairs. It was 'us or them' so we jumped on them. Fighting ensued, more police appeared, and there seemed to be blood everywhere, especially ours. In the end we were over-powered and taken to Wigan Police Station. I soon realised how brutal the police of that day could be; I was badly beaten up in a police cell. The beating was so severe that an ambulance had to be called. The police claimed that I'd fallen downstairs, but there were no stairs at the old station. Here again was another chip on my shoulder, and I was left asking myself, who are the real criminals? Who indeed? Now there was a court case looming, so I had to get my mind ready for that.

Your first offence starts you trembling with fear of the unknown and leaves you wondering how people see you as a person. Before you attend court you are questioned about any other crime you might have committed. In my experience the police are good at feeding your mind with fear. I suppose they use 'the scare you to death treatment', in a hope of deterring you from re-offending. This must work with some, but for others like me this wasn't even a remote possibility. I was too wrapped up in my bitterness towards the police.

My nightmare was about to go deeper. Living Hell was about to begin. By 10.00 am. I was standing in the dock at Wigan Magistrates Court. I was expecting bail and was very relieved to see that Mum and Dad were there. I thought they would speak up for me, but I couldn't have been more wrong. Within five minutes they were telling the magistrate what a problem child I'd been, and how they didn't want to see me again.

The situation was now looking pretty grim. The Judge turned on me insisting that I was no good and didn't deserve my freedom. I managed to shout a few 'obscenities' at him before being handcuffed and dragged off to the cells. I'd assumed prisoner status. He remanded me to Risley Prison for three weeks. In the 1960's Risley was famed for being called Grisly Risley, and I was soon to find out why.

The police escort was bad enough; they couldn't wait to get me to Risley. This was where I had to dig deep into myself, to overcome the fear building up inside me. My mind raced as I frantically tried to get my act together. This was one journey I didn't want to ever make again. I was really on my own now, with no one to turn to, locked up in a Black Mariah Police Van heading towards notorious Grisly Risley.

4.

Doing Time in Risley

As the van drew near the prison gates I felt the pit of my stomach knot up with fear and foreboding, with anticipation of the unknown.   As we pulled into the approach road, the driver gave two hoots on the horn. The prison gates opened with the formidable clanging of heavy metal.

We drove through them to the main office reception area, where I heard the driver shout, "One on for delivery". The vehicle stopped and the rear door opened. There I saw my destination. Two cream coloured, iron doors opened to reveal an intimidating building with dark grey walls. Its appearance alone was enough to fill me with dread.

Two policemen escorted me into the reception area and unlocked my handcuffs. Here I was greeted by three prison officers, known to the inmates as screws.

"Well what have we got here", asked one.

"Myself Squire" I replied. Immediately two of the screws jumped on me kicking, punching, and reminding me I wasn't on holiday. I retaliated with a head butt to one of the screw's faces. Fear and anxiety gripped me. When more screws rushed in to help them, I thought my world had come to an end. However, I survived and was taken to a cell, where I was stripped and put into a bath of cold water. After a while, I was given a brown, scruffy uniform, striped shirt, and shoes that were too big. What was going to happen next? It was such a different world in there and my mind was in a whirl trying to make sense of everything. 24 hours previously I had been a bored youth with a bad attitude, now I was an inmate in prison!

After two or three hours, I was taken for my induction. Two different screws marched me into an office, where I was introduced to a very unwelcoming, grim looking man. He wore a dark suit and was seated behind a desk.

He removed his glasses, looked up to me and enquired with indifference, "What's your name?"

"Les Deane". I replied.

"What's you name?" He repeated a little louder, paying me more attention this time and stubbing out his cigarette.

"Les Deane?" I answered.

"What's your name?" He was almost shouting now, his eyes glaring at me with anger and menace.

"Les Deane". I answered again wondering what was going on. Then I asked him if he was deaf. I had a habit of asking the wrong questions. He had wanted me to say, Les Deane, *Sir*. Two officers grabbed my arms while the grim looking man punched me in the face. I started to go berserk, and was dragged away to a cell.

A screw shouted, "Before long you're gonna to be a broken spirit". From then on I knew why they called this Grisly Risley. I thought, *this is going to be tough, and where's God when you need him?*

I wondered where all this was going to lead. If I had a chip on my shoulder before, then by now it must have grown into a rock, and there were three weeks of this to endure before I went back to court.

At this point I was just a lost person, who was looking for whatever was missing from his life. However, my three weeks seemed a lifetime, and now in my own mind I had to work out who the real criminals were. After I'd been in Risley for ten days my probation officer came to see me. Of course he wanted to know why I was in such a state and so I told him. That night some screws came into my cell and beat me up again.

"So you thought it was clever to tell your probation officer did you", one of them shouted at me. Apparently my probation officer had gone to the regulator, in his own words, to 'stick up for me'. He hadn't considered that there might be repercussions.

On the probation officer's next visit I told him what had happened to me, and showed him my new bruises, adding "Get out; I never want to see you again!"

I had a very bad time in Risley, and three days before I was due back in court I got into a serious fight with a screw. I was so black and blue that my eyes were almost closed. On the Sunday, a day before my court case, another screw came into my cell informing me that I was due back in court the next day. He started shouting at me, but thankfully another inmate, a black guy called Lennox, walked into my cell. He grabbed the screw by the throat, giving him a strong warning. I was astounded because the screw just turned and walked away. Lennox told me just how bad Risley was, but also explained that proper prisons weren't as awful. I later discovered he was going to get a life sentence. I never found out what his crime was and didn't think it wise to enquire.

Monday dawned and I was taken back to court. When my case came up the magistrate took one look at me, and demanded to know why I was in such a state. The prison officer who got up to explain told nothing but lies. He could hardly have told the truth. The magistrate ordered me to be taken back to Risley for one week, emphasising that I must be placed in the hospital wing and treated well. On my arrival back at Risley, I was expecting more of the same; however, they put me straight into the hospital where I was amazed at how well I was treated. Every night I expected someone to come in and give me a good hiding, but to my relief it never happened. This was like a different prison. I was given first class treatment and felt under no threat.

5.

Lightfoot House

The week in hospital passed quickly and my court case was soon in progress. The court probation officer submitted a rather vague probation report to the court, but the magistrate had already made up his mind that I was a violent criminal. Even my parents were disinterested in my freedom. The judge announced that I was to be sent to Lightfoot House, an open prison in Ipswich, for two years. An open prison! I was amazed at my good fortune.

A police officer quickly handcuffed me, and drove me to the railway station, then accompanied me on the long journey from Wigan to Ipswich.

Memories of my beatings at Risley were fresh in my mind, so when we arrived at Lightfoot House I was expecting another beating as part of my induction. Instead, I was marched into reception where I was astonished to find the place looked more like a Hotel.

Once we were inside his office, the Governor made my escort remove the handcuffs then he shook my hand saying, "Welcome." Now I was really worried.

I panicked a bit and started shouting, "Come on, let's get it over with."

Looking shocked, the Governor just responded, "Why don't we have a drink and something to eat?" My mind couldn't stop buzzing around. I was suspicious, why were they being nice to me?

After a while my escort left, and I had to listen to all the rules and regulations before being taken to my cell. Although very small, it was more like a bedroom. There were nice patterned curtains, a proper bed, sheets and a pillow. It all was so different to what I'd been expecting; for one thing everything was clean. Even the other inmates were easy to get on with. We were given slippers, had a great chef, and a menu to choose from each day. I wondered if all this was real. I was still waiting for the bad things to start happening.

After a week, I was told that I was going to work in the flourmill, outside the prison, near the town centre. I would work twelve hours a day, five days a week, and could go out on Saturdays, for six hours, anywhere I wanted. They gave me fifteen pounds spending money too. I thought, *okay, I'll wake up and find myself back in Risley in a minute.*

I also learned that if I absconded I would go to a secure jail for two years, and this would mean no freedom at all.

Inside prison I had plenty of time to reflect on how my life had been, and on the bad decisions and mistakes I'd made. Soon the nightmare of Grisly Risley faded away. My circumstances at Lightfoot House were much better, and I was even feeling settled. I got along with all the other inmates and the staff were very good too. They treated us all like human beings.

The Governor and his wife, Mr. and Mrs. Craig, were strict yet approachable, but it was still a shock when, one Sunday morning, Mr. Craig came into my room dressed in a Salvation Army uniform, and asked if I would like to go with him to the 'Sally Anne' Church. *Wow*, I thought. *No chance.* I was amazed to learn that some of the other inmates did go along. I was beginning to understand how these Half Way

Prisons could be a good influence, although to my thinking you couldn't really call this prison. I could appreciate how a criminal's quality of life could change for the better in a place like this, and the only problem I could foresee was that one-day I would have to leave. It seems a strange thing to say but this thought stirred up sadness in me. Lightfoot House gave me a sense of belonging.

One day the Pastor of a local Pentecostal Church came in to see the Governor. He needed a couple of helpers to do some minor work in his Church. The Governor agreed and I was chosen to go and help out. I thought, *here we go, more ranting on about God.* I went along after work, for a couple of hours, three nights a week and came to know Pastor Cliff, his wife, Eunice, and their children very well. Cliff and Eunice were very friendly and supportive, but I knew their kind of life wasn't for me, or so I thought. What I didn't know then was that God never forgets about you, nor lets you go.

I worked very hard during my time in Lightfoot House, and tried to be like everyone else. Although I did get into a couple of fights, there wasn't anything serious; I was really quite well behaved. When I had problems and life seemed hard, there was someone to talk to, who would show you healthier ways of dealing with life's hardships and problems.

All too soon my time at Lightfoot House was drawing to a close, and my release date was only a few weeks away. I'd had plenty of time to reflect—plenty of time to consider the differences in the world, good and bad—and couldn't say that I'd not been given the chance to go straight, but the stark reality of life on the outside was now staring back at me.

I was sad to be leaving Lightfoot House because in there, there was a safety-gate of people who wanted to encourage me. I'd made many friends too, but most of these were going their own way and I would never see them again.

Once I was released I decided to stay in Ipswich. Within a matter of weeks I met a young lady who seemed to like me a lot, I found a job, and I moved into a one bed roomed flat. What could possibly go wrong? Well, within ten weeks of being free my life seemed empty once more.

I decided to visit my family in Manchester. This went quite well. We were able to go out for a drink, and talk about football just like we used to, but after a week I was fed up and bored, the emptiness having returned, and I was missing my safety gate of friends. It was time to move on again.

I returned to Ipswich. Very soon I lost my job and my girl, and things were looking bleak once more. Memories of Lightfoot House, and all its goodness, were receding into the back of my mind. I headed down to London, sleeping rough for a couple of nights.

I met another girl, Anna, on Victoria Station. She was a prostitute. We went back to her flat, which was small but homely. There was never a relationship between us, but she offered a helping hand and even found me a job in a nearby pub. Here I quickly learned to '*harden up and not take rubbish from anyone*'. Throwing out drunks was part of the job description and a daily occurrence. In this environment you soon found out who your friends were and who would stab you in the back. There were plenty of the latter. I was heading for a downfall.

6.

A Life of Crime

I met up with gangsters from all over London. Some were all right whilst others were vicious swine's, but the common denominator was fear; it ran through all of them.

I always loved playing snooker and spent a lot of time at the snooker table. In later life I became a professional snooker referee, and got to know many well known snooker players, but that wasn't to happen for many years. At this stage, the snooker table was a great place to meet like minded people.

Through one of these contacts I joined up with a particular gang who ran most of the clubs and pubs in the East End of London. They were notorious and ruled with fear. Everyone had to treat these people with respect or risk disappearing for good. There were protection rackets, car scams and there was always money-lending, (known as sharking). There were so many ways money was made, and none of it legal.

In my heart, I don't believe I was a hardened criminal as I always retained a measure of decency. This was brought home to me several times during my 'gangster' days, but especially so in an incident that took place when a colleague and I were sent to a house to collect some money from a young, black couple. They had fallen behind with their repayments to the gang, which wasn't surprising as the interest rate was extortionate. We knocked on their door, and as the woman cautiously opened it we barged inside. Both the man and his wife looked terrified as they didn't have any money to give us.

The couple knew we had orders to hurt them, but I couldn't find it within me to do this. Instead I took the man into the kitchen and instructed my colleague to stay with the wife in the living room.

I shouted in mock anger, "Give me the money or you'll pay for it," and thumped the countertop hard several times, so it would seem to my associate that I was giving the man a good kicking. Then I dug in my pocket and took out two hundred pounds.

"You've paid the money" I said quietly. The man was so grateful. "Now make like you've just been beaten, and be sure you have the money next time." My colleague and I left, and the gang never found out what I'd done.

I learnt to stand up to some extremely nasty people who would shoot you as soon as look at you. I always had to have my wits about me. For example, one chap was, on the surface, the nicest man you could ever want to meet. He spoke to me as if I was a good friend, but I knew that he had no conscience, and if he was given the instruction, he wouldn't hesitate in killing me or anyone else. The police hated and despised these people, which now included me; a certain notoriety came from being associated them.

I was into car theft on a large scale, my run being Ipswich, Norwich and London. Money was flowing and girls were around day and night. It was such a different world, crime upon crime. I was hauled into various police stations and interrogated on many occasions, but it was to no avail. If you 'grassed' on anyone you were literally dead. There was, and still is, fear amongst thieves, and not brotherhood as the film industry would have us believe.

Although the sixties was a great era for music, the late sixties were my nightmare. I was into all types of crime, but give thieves their due, they were mostly interested in jewellery, cars, and money in those days. Compared with crime today, yesterday's criminals were clean. For instance, if a petty criminal had beaten and robbed a frail pensioner, as sometimes happens today, the professional criminals would soon have taught that person a lesson. The criminal world was structured and the real criminals would have been just as keen to catch the offender as the police, although the justice they metered out would have been much harsher and not at all legal.

Any policeman of yesteryear will clarify the contrast with today's criminals. Yesterday's criminals would rob you and leave, but today's will rob, maim, or kill you for just a few pence, or even just for fun. Young or old, pensioners or disabled, it doesn't matter to them. Most seem to have no conscience.

I was eventually brought to justice for burglary and car and jewellery theft, and found myself before Ipswich Crown Court. My life of crime had caught up with me. There had been a police swoop on lots of criminals and I faced a long sentence, the length of which was vastly increased due to my association with certain gang members.

The previous November I'd received three months for car theft and had spent Christmas inside Norwich Prison. Serving three months wasn't too bad—a part of the job description even—but this time my sentence was much longer. I nearly collapsed when the judge gave me twelve years!

He wasn't interested in any sob stories and harshly declared, "Just send him down!"

7.

Norwich Prison

Life wasn't at all pleasant in Norwich Prison, but then it wasn't meant to be.

When you had lived as I had, it was very hard to turn your life around, no matter how many chances you got. There was always a battle raging deep inside me, and I desperately wanted to find the reason for my being the way I was. At that time I was a very frustrated person. I didn't want to be that way and certainly didn't want to live the way I'd been living. I just wanted to be normal and live a normal life.

There is glamour, excitement and fear associated with crime and criminals. Lies and deceit are a way of life, but it's the wrong side of life. You live under the great pretence that every criminal is your friend, and in prison you have the adage, '*it's them and us*', '*them*' being the screws, and '*us*' being the inmates. Because of my involvement with certain infamous criminals I was treated as a celebrity by some of the screws, although never in a positive way. I too had gained notoriety.

The prison staff wanted the inmates to know, in no uncertain terms, that they were in charge and that the inmates were there to be punished. Many times I would be asleep in my cell when two or more screws would barge in and tip the

26

bed over. They would search through my few belongings, leave a right mess, and order me to clean it up. They delighted in *'giving me grief'* so my cell would be *'turned over'* at regular intervals.

I was given duties of scrubbing the floors or toilets, and sometimes of unloading the delivery wagons. This was very hard work indeed and you were 'kept at it' with very little rest. Once I was placed to work in the laundry. This was a step up, almost like a promotion, and I earned two pounds fifty pence a week.

I and two other inmates shared a cell with only one potty between us. The beds were very uncomfortable, and the blankets dirty. You had to watch your back, as you couldn't trust anyone. I came up against many problems. Suicide was always an option to us all and I saw some pitiful sights. In prison the one thing you have to remember is that it's *your* fault that you are inside. I met lifers, murderers, rapists, muggers and people who were just in for non-payment of fines. You never forget the individual scenes.

One such instance was when Peter was placed in my cell. He was a very scared and withdrawn young man, with loads of problems including a violent temper. I learned that he was serving three years for violent crime. As soon as I met him I knew he was going to be trouble. Oddly enough, we got on well. Each morning when the cell door was opened, all the inmates had to take their potties to the long sink on the landing to empty and wash them out. Most days, Peter would stand naked in that sink which was, by then, filled with urine and excretion; his problem ran very deep. No one bothered with him, except for every now and then when the Chaplain would come and try to speak with him. Even so, one day Peter attempted suicide and nearly succeeded. He was rushed to a Psycho Ward and I never saw him again.

Norwich Prison had cabin huts in its grounds holding up to twelve prisoners in each. One day I was moved to Hut Two. This was supposed to be a privilege; however, it's a fact of prison life there is always one inmate who dominates the rest. This person was in my hut and was known as Scotch Eddie. He was a very hard case and was serving five years. It was my fortune to get on with him very well, but there were others there that you had to keep your eye on. It's in this situation you start to realise what being a criminal is all about.

Night times were spent sitting around a coal fire frying bacon and eggs stolen from the kitchen earlier the same day. Sometimes a screw would walk in and join you; they were as bad as us.

Work started at 7.30 am. and finished at 4.30 pm., when letters from friends and loved ones would arrive. The expressions on the cons' faces always gave away who had received nice letters, and who'd got the bad ones known as 'Dear Johns'. A 'Dear John' was the letter from a wife or girlfriend letting the recipient know that she had met someone else, or that she wanted nothing more to do with him.

Sometimes, just once a month for twenty minutes, you might have a visit from a friend or relative. I'd seen hardened criminals break down and cry after visits and didn't want to go through that myself. I knew that seeing friends or family would remind me of my loss of freedom, so I told everyone not to come. They respected my wish and no one came.

I started to feel the pressure of being in prison for a long stretch. It was like this was the whole of your life and the world outside no longer existed. I would have loved to have a lie in just one morning a week, but there was no chance of that.

In prison everyone is wary of everyone else. There is no trust. You aren't even allowed to think for yourself. As a result you start to daydream. You build up a very clear picture of how your life will be when you get out, but it's only a dream—a fantasy—I'm afraid reality sees to that. You also build up a rapport with the other inmates and the officers, but still always remain on guard. In reality, you are always on your own.

An ugly situation can soon materialise between inmates, and between inmates and screws. I witnessed many ugly situations. I saw inmates mentally crack up. Depression affected everyone. There were bullies amongst the cons, and always a baron, the one who ruled a certain wing. Even the screws didn't bother the baron. Many times I wished that my life had gone in a different direction. Why did I still always have this empty feeling? My father had always told me what a hard worker I was and couldn't understand why I'd turned to crime. I was definitely the 'black sheep' of the family, my brothers and sisters were all living fairly good lives.

After had been inside for around nine months I was called to the governor's office, where I was offered a choice of work detail outside the prison walls. There were lots of weeds that needed pulling up.

I explained to the Governor, "No way, I'll be on my toes and do a runner. I've got unfinished business on the outside; I'll escape".

"No, you're a good lad" he replied, "I know you're not the sort to go on the run". How wrong he was. He didn't listen to my objections and put me on the outside work detail anyway. On my first day, after no longer than two hours I 'did a runner.'

There were about twelve of us in the outside work party, but only one officer to supervise. We were all allocated different work areas. The officer in charge of the work detail told two of us to go to the section near the main road to weed and generally clean up the area. When he was out of sight checking on some other inmates I spotted a lorry coming towards us. I stuck out my right hand and thumbed a lift.

The lorry stopped and the driver wound down his window.

"Where you going mate?" He asked.

"Ipswich" I replied. He gestured me to join him in his lorry, which I promptly did, and off we went. My prison uniform was hidden beneath my overalls so he never suspected that I was one of the inmates, even though he picked me up outside the prison.

An hour or so later I was standing outside a friend's flat in Ipswich. You see, I had to deal with Michael, the guy who had 'grassed me up.'

Within two days I'd traced him to a nightclub just outside the town. As soon as he spotted me he darted across the room and '*jumped on me*'. The next few moments were a confusion of fists flying, and head butting culminating in the two of us crashing through a table and glasses smashing on the ground. A couple of bouncers grabbed us both and threw us out into the street, where I continued to beat the daylights out of Michael. The fracas resulted in me gaining a few cuts and bruises, but Michael faired much worse; he suffered a broken nose, a broken arm and a busted lip. The police were called, but before they arrived I managed to slip away.

I hurried to a house in Hossack Road where some other friends lived. They helped me for two days, and then I left for the train station, intending to visit some people in Colchester whom I knew would help me avoid recapture.

While I was on the platform waiting for my train, I noticed a police car pull up with four policemen inside. They got out and walked onto the platform. I tried to remain calm and inconspicuous. Then a police van drew up right outside the doorway to the train station. I knew they had come for me, so I casually made my way through the crowd, off the platform and back onto the street, where I watched from the corner. The police came out and stood at the front of the station looking all around, so I quietly made my way down the main street, climbed over a fence, and through a couple of gardens to knock them off my trail.

When I reached the shopping center, I took a short cut through Woolworths. As I was passing the gents clothing section I turned to see two CID men approaching.

"Don't put a fight up Les" the first one said. They knew me by name. I didn't struggle; I'd already done what I'd come to do. I was arrested, handcuffed and bustled into the back of a police car. Soon I found myself inside a cell at Ipswich police station.

Two police officers came down to see me. They were quite cordial.

"Did you enjoy Ipswich then? Norwich not good enough for you?" one of them asked.

"Not keen on the facilities there" I joked.

I spent twenty four hours in the cell, before being escorted back to Norwich Prison.

The entrance of the prison had two gates, spaced around twenty feet apart, with an office situated in-between, and was bordered on each side by a high wired fence. Usually on arrival the two gates opened simultaneously and you were driven straight through into the main gate yard, but this time the car stopped in the area between the gates and the gate in front remained closed. I heard the familiar clang of metal as gate behind me slammed shut, and I was told to get out of the car. My escorting officer went into the office, signed the papers to acknowledge that he had released me back into prison custody, and then made his way back to the car.

"You'd better watch out now Les" He warned me, "this is where things'll get difficult for you." He got back in the police car and drove away leaving me in the holding area.

I looked around. Between me and the second gate were six prison officers standing in a line, three on either side of the reception area. As I walked between them they stared kicking me and striking me with their truncheons.

"This is what 'appens to people like you," one of them snarled at me, his eyes filled with hate and contempt. I was taken to main reception bruised and bleeding, then striped, and thrown into a bath of cold water. I had to wear a different uniform this time, a grey jacket, and trousers with a narrow yellow stripe running down the outside of both trouser legs. This was to show everyone that I was an escapee. I was told I would wear that uniform for six months, but the respect I gained from the other prisoners lasted much longer.

Unfortunately I lost the privilege of staying in the huts and was relocated back inside the main prison building. Once in my cell two more screws barged in and roughed me up again.

During the next communal meal time there were shouts of "Well done" and "Have a pie on me" from the other inmates.

The next day I was taken to see the Governor who assured me that this would be the first and only time I would escape. I lost seven days remission, and was told I was to work in the building department unloading incoming heavy goods vehicles.

The screws made me work very hard. One day soon after my recapture, a lorry came in carrying four tonnes of salt and sugar, all in hundred weight sacks. These sacks all had to be off-loaded by hand. I and a few other cons were instructed to carry them up two flights of stairs, and stack them on pallets. After we had carried and stacked about three tonnes I was ordered to carry the remaining sacks by myself.

I was already exhausted. Half way through the task my shoulders were already red-raw and perspiration was running down my face, but I still had to find the strength to lift and carry each sack. With each step I had to draw deep within myself to find the strength to continue. I've never known two flights of stairs to seem so long. The screws could see how weak I was and how much I was struggling. My legs and back ached with pain, but the cons in my group weren't allowed to help, they could only watch.

Whenever I became too tired and looked like I was slowing down the screw would shout, "Move you slime!" and poke me with a truncheon.

Eventually through sheer determination I got to the last sack. I was exhausted and felt faint, but I managed to carry that sack and stack it.

All the cons cheered and shouted, "Well done!", and "Don't let the b....... grind you down!" I noticed that I'd won a little respect from the screws and definite admiration from the other cons.

After a month had passed I was placed back in barracks, the proper name for the huts. In some ways I'd surprised myself with my new found good behaviour and I felt good inside. I still wore my escapee uniform. Although some of the screws were okay about this, others hated anyone in this uniform and let me know about it in no uncertain terms. Five months later I was given a normal prison uniform.

One thing you realize in prison is that the system stinks. You are a nothing, only a number. Each prisoner has the same fear and the only thing to look forward to is your release. Until then you watch your back.

Some time later I had to attend a workshop in 'C Wing' to spend a few hours making cardboard boxes. Somewhat out of character, I got talking to a Prison Work Officer. I couldn't stand the system, the 'them and us' scenario was very strongly engraved into my mind set.

During this short discussion he asked me, "Do you believe in God?" I thought, *I'm going to punch this fellow on the nose.*

"What a question", I replied purposely keeping both hands firmly fixed in my pockets, "I'm in jail and you ask that".

"Well I do and I'll pray for you" *What a cheek* I thought. I felt annoyed at what I considered to be impertinence, but didn't know then that God hadn't forgotten me.

In any prison of this time, fear was an unrelenting fact of life, while physical and mental abuse was a daily issue. Punishment and threats came in many forms from prison wardens and inmates alike. I've seen 'first time' inmates scream with fear, and on many occasions have witnessed sexual abuse in the showers. The prison officers offered no assistance to the victim, but simply disappeared as soon as it started, and unless you wanted the same treatment yourself, or worse, you could do nothing to help.

One of my more horrific experiences occurred at about eleven o'clock one night while all the prisoners were locked up. I heard a screw unlocking and opening my cell door. He ordered me out into the corridor and handcuffed me to the stair rails.

Barricaded inside the cell next to mine were three young men who were protesting to an injustice they felt they had received from the system. Six more screws were hastily summoned. They came rushing down the corridor to force entry to the cell with a special jack. The first screw unlocked my handcuffs and threw me back inside my cell, slamming and locking my door.

I heard banging and shouting going back and forth between the screws and the inmates. Suddenly their door crashed open and the officers charged in. Panic, fear, and violence followed. I heard the prisoners screaming, "Get off me... get off" and sounds of violence coming from the officers. Then I heard a key being turned in my cell door. I froze, wondering if I was going to be next.

A screw coarsely shouted at me, "Deane, get out 'ere". I obeyed and was shown into the now empty cell next to mine. I looked around at the blood splattered walls and excrement covered floor. It looked liked a scene from a horror movie, and the stench was overpowering. The screw left me for a moment, so I walked back to the cell doorway and peered through it, taking a few welcome gulps of fresh air. I saw the three inmates being dragged away, whilst the screws rained down blow upon blow on their victims with their truncheons. The screws still didn't relent but kicked the blood-covered inmates down the iron stairs, on their way to another block. The chief officer turned to face me starring with hate filled eyes.

"You bloody hard cases... we'll break you! Now get a bucket and mop and clean this mess up!" It was a mess too, but so were those inmates. They didn't stand a chance and no mercy was shown. The next day I learned that they had broken arms and legs and were covered in bruises. Of course they were quickly transferred to another prison and I never saw them again. I had nightmares for two weeks afterwards, but the inmates' screams of terror and pain haunted me for years to come.

The next day a principal officer came to my cell and spoke to me in a quiet yet very intimidating manner, "You never saw anything. Remember this if you know what's good for you."

Now certain screws 'had it in' for particular inmates, and if the inmates tried to stand their ground with those screws, trouble followed. In those days prison life was very tough and at times morally wrong. I'm not saying that we didn't deserve punishment but there are limits. Today inmates would complain about their human rights, and rightly so, but the 1960's afforded us no such luxury. Some screws loved to use fear to gain the psychological advantage.

One such screw was famously known to us inmates as 'the singing screw'. He always worked the night shift, and would walk around playing his guitar and singing. Suddenly he'd stop and you'd hear a cell door being opened, followed by screaming as the inmate was beaten up. Many nights I lay in bed listening to 'the singing screw' getting closer and closer, hoping that he didn't stop singing outside my cell door. When he passed by I breathed a sigh of relief, knowing I was at least safe for the time being.

One night I definitely I did the wrong thing. I was fed up of a particular night screw constantly bullying weaker cons, so I threatened him.

I starred into his eyes and said firmly, "If you touch another con I'll smack you up!" He didn't respond, but silently walked away. I should have known better than to think I'd got away with speaking to a screw like that.

At about three o'clock in the morning my cell door opened, and the screw ordered my two cell mates to go to the toilets. When they left three more screws rushed in, grabbing at me roughly and dragging me off the bed. They threw a mattress on top of me and pinned me down, so I was unable to fight back or defend myself. It covered me from my head to my thighs. Then they struck me repeatedly across my legs and feet with their truncheons. Again and again the blows rained down.

"Keep your thoughts to yourself in future" one screw growled at me. I was left bruised and bleeding once more. In the report it stated that I'd fallen down the stairs, another 'fit up'.

Crime does not pay! I am so thankful that somehow God had his hand on my life; many times I feared death was only a heart beat away. In prison and frequently afterwards, living amongst all that fear and hate, I considered life very unfair. I used to see normal people getting on in life, and ask myself why I couldn't live like they did.

During these two years, prison life had had a drastic effect on me. This was because I couldn't see the end; I didn't believe I would ever leave. I became full of fear and anxiety and became a 'snapper', that is, my temper grew much worse. If a screw moved towards me I would think he was going to assault me, so I would hit out at him before he hit me, even though, in reality, he wasn't going to touch me. In prison I witnessed so much more violence than I had ever encountered on the streets in my gangland days.

Six weeks into my third year I was ordered to go to see the Governor. I was nervous to say the least, as I didn't want to be transferred to another prison, but this time it was good news. The Governor told me that the appeal against my sentence was at last to be heard in Ipswich Crown Court.

Finally my day came. I was nervous, as I knew my case could go either way, but my barrister spoke very well and my sentence was reduced to five years. This meant that I wouldn't have long to wait until I was free. If I'd lost the appeal I would have had to start my sentence again and serve the twelve years minus any remission I'd earned.

This was the case of an inmate that I knew. He had served four years of a nine-year sentence when he lost his appeal and had to start the sentence again from the beginning. Imagine that! In all, he had to serve thirteen years instead of the original nine, just because his appeal was turned down.

As can often be the case, by now I'd developed a fear of coming out of prison. *What sort of life would await me? Would I end up back inside?* All these thoughts and many more were turning around and around in my mind. Soon my daydreams of freedom became a nightmare. I could understand how people became institutionalised, not wanting to leave prison. Fear of the unknown made it feel safer on the inside.

Well my release date arrived and I was finally leaving. I said my goodbyes to the other inmates, and the Governor wished me all the best. As I walked through the first gate and past the reception area a diversity of emotions were welling up inside me: fear, happiness, excitement, desperation and I was wondering, *what's outside there for me?* Finally I was standing in front of the main gates and the warden was opening the door. At last I saw freedom. I felt freedom. I smelt freedom. I walked forward, breathed in the fresh air and gazed upwards. The clear blue sky looked beautiful. I was out!

* * *

As I walked up the main street towards Norwich, a black car, a Jaguar, pulled up at my side. The driver wound down his window.

"Hiya", he said demanding my attention, "We need to chat". There was something definitely ominous about this situation. A heavy-set, rough looking man of my previous acquaintance stepped out of the passenger side and offered me a lift.

"That's alright I can walk" I told him, trying to appear confident. I guessed who had sent them.

"It's better that you get in. We need to have a chat" he insisted sounding more threatening than polite. I knew better than to refuse, so I climbed into the back of the car, which hastily sped off, with me now sitting between two of my old 'friends.' A sawn-off shotgun was pointing in my direction. My mind was juggling all my thoughts and fear, *was this the end, or should I at least put up a fight to get out?* I pictured my dead body being thrown out of the car and knew I'd only seconds to act. I reasoned that I could grab the gun, push it down to the floor, and kick the driver so he'd swerve or crash the car. Maybe this would cause enough of a diversion for me to escape.

We were nearing the train station. Before I could put my plan into action, Jeff, the henchman on my left, said, "From now on you stay clear of London, Norwich and Ipswich". He thrust a brown envelope into my hands containing five hundred pounds, and they let me go.

8.

A Glimmer of Hope

The money I received was just a hand out, but I really needed it. Although I'd been told to stay away from London, Norwich and Ipswich, I knew from experience that those who had given me the warning meant that I wasn't to commit any crimes in these places. I would be alright staying in Ipswich if I kept on the right side of the law, so this is what I decided to do.

It had been frightening coming out of prison. I felt insecure. I had to report to a Probation Officer to let him know where I was, and if I needed any help, although I didn't believe he'd want to help anyway. Next I had to go to the local Social Security Office to show them my Release Papers, and collect my seventy-one pounds release allowance. Although it wasn't a lot, it was enough to secure a one-room bed-sitter. I also found a job working nights in a local foundry in Lacton, Ipswich. It was a dirty job, but I believed that if I worked nights, and slept during the day, there would be little time in which to get into trouble. I was very pleased with myself; I'd just been released and landed on my feet.

By the time I'd been working at the foundry for six weeks I'd done my little bed-sitter up very nicely. It was homely and I was as they say, '*as snug as a bug in a rug*'. I was very pleased at how I was settling down, and I'd also made one or two friends along the way. Most importantly, I didn't want to be a criminal any more. I was feeling optimistic and believed success could be around the corner, although I still had nightmares about my prison experience, and would often wake up in a hot sweat realising how near to death I'd been.

By contrast, when a young man is on his feet he looks to a bright and wonderful future. He builds up dreams in his mind, such as being married with a few children, and owning his own house. I wanted to be that young man; I wanted this to be my reality.

There were times when I looked back and tried to make sense of my life. I remembered the situations I'd been in, the bad criminals I'd met, and the foolishness I'd got myself into. I knew that if I'd been less immature back then, my life would have turned out differently. I'd no one to blame but myself. Although it wasn't perfect, I was brought up in a respectable family and compared to some of the other cons, mine had been a pretty decent upbringing.

I asked myself all kinds of questions but couldn't find the answers. The fact was I'd chosen to be a criminal. I chose my path during those early years. Now, I can thank God that I came away from it. Prison life is not a life; it's not even living and it's certainly not God's plan, as I was to find out in later life. I met so many criminals inside and outside of prison, and felt such fear and violence; the likes of which I never dreamed existed in this world. Judges say that there is law and lawlessness. Sometimes, in situations such as those I'd experienced, it was hard to differentiate between the two, but the truth is, we do all know the difference between good and evil, kindness and unkindness.

Since coming out of prison I'd '*landed on my feet*'. I was still in my twenties and had plenty to look forward to. I met a good-looking girl and started a relationship with her. How different life was now compared with my previous years. It seemed so uncomplicated and very enjoyable. Yes, at that moment I was on 'Easy Street'. My girl, Susan, moved in with me. She was a dream come true—tall and very slim, with long blond hair and blue eyes—and most importantly she liked me for who I was. I was happy at last. We built up a circle of friends; this was the kind of life I wanted. At last my dream was coming true, or so I thought. Working the night shift wasn't doing our relationship any favours; in fact it was becoming a strain. I asked to be put to work days, but was told that I would have to wait for a vacancy which could take months.

9.

Shattered Dreams

They say that all good things must come to an end. I didn't know if that cliché was true, but one morning I came home from my nightshift work to find that my dreams had been shattered.

I arrived home at the usual time, just before 7.00 am. As I opened the door I thought the bed-sitter seemed unusually quiet.

I walked in saying something like, "Hi, It's only me". I was feeling very tired and couldn't wait to get to bed; my sweetheart would be there to cuddle up to. It was at these times that I didn't mind working nights.

However, I was in for a shock. There was a note waiting for me on the kitchen table. It contained very few words:

I'm sorry but I've found someone else
—Susan

I just sat down, my mind refusing to believe the words in front of me. Suddenly, panic filled my whole body as I struggled to grasp a hold of reality and the truth that lay before me. It couldn't be true. It just wasn't possible.

Susan had left me just when I thought I'd finally made it in life. I believed that I'd found the missing piece I'd always been seeking. I had that spectacular feeling you get when you find your soul mate, that someone you love and who loves you back. I considered her my closest friend and partner, she was someone I could turn to in the midst of bad times, that special someone I would spend the rest of my life with. I thought Susan would fill the emptiness I'd always felt, but I'd become vulnerable, and in throwing my heart on the line, the pain I now felt within was even more immense and unbearable than the void itself.

I decided then that I wasn't born to be like normal people. It was like everything around me was false. I was so disappointed. Where had I gone wrong? In frustration, I smashed up my home. I needed answers, my biggest question being *why*?

I went looking for her, my mind still racing with a thousand thoughts. Surely we could work something out. I found her, but it was true, she had met someone else. Jealousy gripped me.

I just asked her, "Why... what was wrong with us being together?"

"My life is so boring! You're out all night and sleep all day, and we never go out together any more!" I felt let down and dreadfully hurt. "It's too late to change now", she continued, "I'm happy with this other guy".

I walked away, devastated, deciding to pack my job in and leave town. I was running away from my problems again.

I headed to Manchester and visited my family, but they still held me at arms length. I noticed I was drinking and smoking heavily, talking the usual rubbish, and feeling empty again.

It's surprising how your circumstances can change so quickly: your livelihood, your happiness, and your whole existence. Inside you can be hurting and can be an emotional mess, but you wear a false mask pretending that everything is all right.

"How y' doing?" People ask.

"Oh, I'm okay", you answer, but deep inside you're quite the opposite. I had to make a big decision, a life changing decision. Nobody, not even my family, expected anything good to happen in my life. Whenever I visited any of my relations I could feel how unwelcome I was.

One of them told me, "the road is long with many a winding turn". They were right; change was just around the corner.

One evening I went into The Albion, a Pub where most of my family gathered each night. As I sat there, listening to all the conversations of how each one was getting along, I felt such a huge gap between them and me. I thought, *hey, I'm the one with the big personality, cheerful, always joking and doing all the impressions, yet I'm the odd one out.* I'd made my decision. After I left the pub I was going to drop out of society. Enough was enough; I just wanted to be alone to find that missing part of my life.

I continued my thoughts, *when I go I'll just walk and walk.* I gave no consideration to how I would eat or drink. Who cared anyway?

10.

Life on the Streets

I walked out of the pub and into an unknown future. My first night under the stars was very cold and lonely, I must admit. It was late September and soon it would be much colder. I needed a drink, anything would do. I soon found this a very tiring, weary way of life, and quickly withdrew into myself.

Self-pity knocked at the door, and '*I couldn't care less*' soon followed. This was my induction as a tramp. I had with me a carrier bag with some underwear and a few pairs of socks, but they didn't last me long. I didn't make a conscious decision to become a tramp, it just sort of happened. Now I had to learn to survive or die. Alone on the streets, you talk to yourself and get very hungry. I found doorways, park benches, and old cars, anywhere to put my head down. *Oh for a comfy bed!* I was a poor learner; I'd only been on the road a week and was already moaning. This life was hard but I was determined to survive.

I'd never considered the life of tramps before, but now I was getting first hand experience. I had to find out how these people survived, for instance, what was their main source?

Ten days slowly passed, during which time I'd only eaten a few scraps on two occasions. It was two o'clock on a bitterly cold night, and I was trudging the streets of Wigan starving, thirsty and very cold. Standing by the Old Market in the centre of town, just a few hundred yards from my first crime, brought back so many bad memories.

A hand on my shoulder startled me, quickly bringing me back to the present, and a rough voice said, "Hey, you hungry?"

"Famished". I replied.

The man, clearly a seasoned tramp, continued, "Well let's collect some food".

"How?"

"Easy, you just have to know were to look; they swept up after the market closed. In the corners and dustbins you'll find all the vegetable waste they dumped". I reluctantly peered into a dustbin, while the tramp rummaged around inside another one. "Look", he said, "Half a cabbage, some onions, and carrots." This stranger was a fully-fledged tramp, and boy did he smell, but he knew how to survive. We collected our vegetables and walked to a derelict house where two other tramps had already lit a fire in the fireplace.

It was only a small fire, made up of sticks and rubbish, but it had warmed the room. We poured water into an empty can, broke up the vegetables—adding them to the water—and carefully placed the can on the fire to boil. The first tramp pulled out a bottle, containing an awful tasting mixture of wine and cider they called scrumpy, and poured some of the concoction over the vegetables. When you're as hungry as I was you'll eat anything. After about thirty minutes he removed the can, and gave me an old tin lid.

"That's your spoon", he said allowing me the first taste. The food was rough but welcome to my stomach. It felt good to get something inside me at last.

I'd learned a valuable lesson: how to eat whatever and not be fussy. I was also learning to beg and steal to survive. My education as a tramp was growing but the loneliness was overwhelming. Life was never a holiday. The police didn't like tramps and would move us on and on. In those days they just didn't want to know.

At this early stage I could have left the streets behind, stopped being a tramp, and returned back to 'normality' relatively easily, but what for? There wasn't anything to go back to. I'd experienced a life of crime, tasted prison life, been involved with a woman and worked hard: none of which had worked out. Everything at this time in my life seemed false. I hadn't found the secret of life. Perhaps other people could cope, but I couldn't. At least in becoming a tramp I didn't have to answer to anyone else; there were no responsibilities. As time passed by I realised I was fooling myself. I was only running away from my problems again, cutting friends, family and everyone else out of my life.

There were very few good times living on the streets. Many tramps I met had similar stories to mine. Some were very educated, but because of various bad experiences they chose to drop out of life. Living rough was very hard, and not many people cared about you.

My first year as a tramp was an education in itself, but it gave me a greater understanding of people, especially the poor. I often wondered how long I was going to live this way, and when I would be able to feel what I wanted to feel. I never realised that worse was to come; I was sinking lower. I'd come to rely on booze. Any kind would do and would help me to sleep. It's hard to sleep when you're freezing cold and often soaking wet. The booze numbed me from the cold. I was begging to buy cheap wine or cider, and looking in the gutter for scraps to eat and cigarette butts to smoke. I was becoming very smelly; my clothes were filthy, and any kind of sensible reasoning had deserted me. There was no return, no going back. My reason for living had deteriorated, although this wasn't living, it was barely an existence.

You might think that because you drop out of society your life stops. It does in regard to the normal style of life, but another life begins. Necessity dictates that you become a beggar, and if you're going to survive you have to become very selfish. Normal-living people look upon you as inferior, '*low life scum*', and no one is interested in why you became a tramp, although there are many different reasons why people do. I spoke to many tramps and found most of their life stories to be very sad, yet on the streets there is also mystery, and occasionally some funny times which can bring a smile to your face.

One of those funny times was when I met two other tramps called Tom and Jeremy. Straight away their names made me smile; I called them Tom and Jerry. The three of us spent a whole week sharing park benches in Chorley Park. One night, when we hadn't eaten or had a hot drink for three days, I came up with a great plan.

"Food" I declared. "Its time for a hot meal."

Tom and Jerry looked at me as if I'd totally lost the plot. Tom asked, "Where? It's three in the morning!" I reminded them about the pond in the park. It had ducks.

"We can light a fire and have roast duck" I explained. A gleam came into their eyes.

"Yes", they cried, "Let's catch a duck!" Well this was easy to say, but it turned out to be virtually impossible. Off we went to catch that duck. My plan was to throw a dirty blanket over one of the ducks swimming on the pond, and in its confusion I reasoned that it would try to fly off and get trapped in the blanket. What a funny sight we must have been: three very determined tramps chasing a duck, with a blanket, in the moonlight. But, you know, ducks aren't that stupid. When we threw the blanket over the duck it moved. Tom jumped in the pond to grab the duck, but it bobbed under

48

the water and swam out to the middle of the pond. Our bellies rumbled and our hearts sank, but not all was lost. Whilst walking around the shops at 5.30 that morning we heard some beautiful sounds, a milk float delivering milk to doorsteps and bread vans delivering their orders to the shops. We managed to steal two loaves, four pints of milk and some newspapers. We had food at last, and newspapers to stuff down our clothes to insulate us against the cold. You do learn to survive: you have to.

In this country we have four seasons in every year, yet few months are warm and welcoming to those living on the streets. When you are one of those unfortunates you really feel the cold and the loneliness, especially as you walk past cafés and see everyone eating and drinking. At such times I would wait and watch to see if a customer left anything on his plate, such as a piece of bacon or toast, and then, if I was lucky, I would nip in and take what was left before the waitress cleared it away. Most times this didn't work out, but when it did, oh what a feast that scrap of food was.

I must have walked thousands of miles in my time, my feet sore and my body weary. There were so many sad times. I questioned the existence of God and whether He was '*up there*' watching me. After all, if He existed, why He didn't help me? I was desperate to make sense of my life.

When I met other tramps, or the short term homeless, the variety of conversations we had were so educational and enlightening, although the reasons they became drop outs usually remained a mystery. I met ex doctors, ex teachers, ex soldiers, young and old, male and female, all living as I was, it was all so sad.

One December's night at around 11.45 pm. it started snowing. The snow flakes were small and hard and stung as the wind blew them into my face. I had big holes in my shoes, no socks and my clothes were soaking wet. It was a few days before Christmas, and I was walking around the shops feeling very unwell. I was literally shaking from the cold. I made the decision to visit Pam, one of my sisters who lived nearby.

As I stood outside her house, peeping through a gap in her curtains, I could see that she was sitting up watching television. I knocked on the door and she invited me in. Her home was warm and cosy. All I wanted was a good night's sleep. I felt embarrassed at my appearance, being so dirty and un-kept. She made me a cup of tea and some lovely toast. It was so good.

She asked, "What's up with you, why'd you live like you do?"

"I don't know" I replied. How could I give a better answer? My health was failing, and I felt so unwell and depressed. At one o'clock that morning she asked me to leave placing a pound in my hand. I thanked her for that, but at the same time I could see that I wasn't welcome. Tears welled up filling my eyes; I felt I'd let her down as well as myself.

That night, if I'd been offered the help, I would have left the streets and tried to start rebuilding my life. Instead, I slept on a bench in the bus station. At least it was dry there, albeit very windy. I was shaking with the cold and feeling such self-pity. I realised that I'd destroyed myself. What a downfall.

"God where are you?" I cried audibly. On hearing no answer I thought, *another day, another hunger pain.*

11.

Alcoholic Syndrome

There were to be many nights like the last one; self-pity had really settled in. I'd learnt how to get my booze by jumping over pub walls, and filling bottles with whatever I could from the dregs left in the bottom of the bottles stacked in the yard: drops of mild bitter, drops of anything. I'd also learned how to mix wine with cider and mentholated spirits. By now I was a real alcoholic, but then who cared? Who was bothered? I was my own worst enemy.

My time on the streets had taught me how to beg money more successfully, and how to keep warm at night by shoving loads of newspaper down my shirt and trousers. Yes, I was becoming a fully-fledged tramp. My hair had grown really long and my beard was wild. I looked a total freak. If you were outside eating chips or a sandwich I would be waiting nearby in case you dropped something. Searching dustbins and waste bins for food and drink had long since become a way of life.

By thumbing eight lifts, I eventually managed to get myself to Felixstowe. Hitch hiking, as a tramp, was very hard as not many people wanted to offer you a lift, and those that did only took you a short distance before dropping you off. Occasionally, some would even give you a few shillings, which was very kind.

In Felixstowe I met a dropout called Harry. He was seventy-nine years old and very experienced. Soon he was showing me good places to sleep and also the art of 'Garden Hopping', which consisted of creeping into gardens late at night to steal blankets or clothing off the washing lines. Things were beginning to get a little better for me, so I was feeling more optimistic. Deciding to freshen up a bit, I took some soap from a gent's toilet, ventured down to the pebbled beach, and had a fabulous wash in the sea. It felt wonderful. My hair hadn't been washed for three years so a good scrub did both it and me good.

That same night I managed to 'acquire' a pair of jeans and a shirt from a caravan site, so this was a good week for me. I'd scrounged around thirty-one pounds in total, and eaten and drank every day. Despite this, my health was still very poor. I was weak and coughing up blood and was beginning to wonder how long I could go on. I imagined someone finding me lying in a ditch or under a hedge: dead.

Winters are bad whenever you are on the streets, or just sleeping rough. Back then, in the 1970's, outside help such as soup kitchens and handouts from the 'Sally Anne' (the Salvation Army) were scarce. Any alcoholic drink was welcome, as you needed this to deaden your feeling for the cold, and there were, of course, the usual camp fires where alcoholics met and shared their grumbles and also a laugh or two. You needed to dig deep into yourself to find your sense of humour, and you always needed to sleep with 'one eye open', otherwise you woke up minus your socks and shoes.

One time I wandered into Ipswich Police Station at two o'clock in the morning asking for a bed for the night. Sometimes the police were helpful and gave you a note to take round to the Sally Anne who ran a '*doss house*' for unfortunates.

On your arrival, you gave them your police note, which secured you a bed for one night and breakfast in the morning. Inside the Sally Anne there was one large hall room with forty beds next to each other, and it stank rotten. No one undressed for bed as you had to sleep with your clothes on or loose them. I was given one sheet and a blanket, and was shown to an empty bed. I lay on it listening to the noises of humanity all around me: coughing, people urinating in their potties, loud snoring, muttering and other horrible noises. At least that night I was comfortable and warm.

At 7.30 the next morning, I was awoken and ushered into another hall, where I lined up with the other street people eagerly awaiting their bacon, egg, bread and cups of tea, poured from a huge urn. By 8.30 am. we were all back out on the cold, wet streets. Still, I couldn't moan at that little bit of kindness. An onlooker would see all the homeless people walking out of the Sally Anne clutching their bottles of wine or cider, their pockets stuffed full of bread.

These down-and-outs once led good, normal lives, but something had turned them into tramps. Once someone's much loved baby, they had now become nobody's child; each one had a story to tell, each one had feelings. I'd managed to see humanity through a different window, and still wondered if there was a God. Did He see us? I really needed to know.

Desperation and uncertainty were always at the forefront of my mind during my time as a tramp. I never knew when or where I would get my next meal, and I really panicked when I couldn't get hold of an alcoholic drink.

Over the next few weeks my 'luck' began to change as I became more successful in begging for money, and occasionally I found some work doing odd jobs, such as gardening or cleaning, if I asked at the right doors. My efforts would often be rewarded with a few sandwiches and a couple of pounds, which would mean I could buy more cider or cheap wine. I always hoped the sun would shine on me, but usually it seemed not to. By now I was getting used to days when nothing went right.

I had one terrible week when it rained everyday and was very cold. At night I was soaking wet and my feet were so cold that they were really hurting. It was very late and the streets were deserted. I was wondering around the town centre, when I suddenly noticed I was standing outside some gents' toilets. They were always locked at that time of night, but I managed to break the lock and cautiously ventured inside. Of course I felt scared that if I got caught I would go back to jail, but in the circumstances this mightn't have been such a bad outcome. At least I'd be warm then, and wouldn't have these terrible hunger pains.

I found a small office which was also locked, so I kicked the door and it flew open. Inside I found lots of dry towels and a small electric fire which I plugged in and turned on. Now I was able to dry myself out and rest for a while in the warm. I also put my clothes in the hand drier to dry them off. Being off the streets and resting for those couple of hours was such a wonderful feeling. There was an electric kettle too and tea bags, but no milk. Never mind, a hot drink was in the offing.

I opened a draw and found three pounds that came in very handy too. After a while my clothes were almost dry, and I was warmed up and ready to face the streets again, so in the early hours I left my warm shelter and went on my way. Later that day I used the money to buy a meat and potato pie and a mug of coffee. This wouldn't seem much to anyone else, but to the man on the street it was a banquet.

Statistically down and outs are very unusual, but not everyone is kind and understanding to them. When you're homeless some people slate you, and others even threaten you with violence. It's not unusual for someone to *put the boot in*. I've even heard of a tramp being burned alive by some youths, who later said they did it just for a laugh. One time I noticed a group of men walking home drinking and eating chips. They were clearly already drunk. Laughing, they discarded their chips and bottle of booze on a low wall. A tramp eagerly walked across the street and started to eat the chips, but the men turned around and cruelly beat him up.

You would expect women to have more compassion for unfortunates, but this isn't necessarily the case. There was a time when I asked a woman if she could spare some loose change and she spat in my face. I walked away thinking, *'I'm glad I'm not as low as her.'*

Some ministers that I came across were a little better.

I asked one if he could spare some change, but he said, "Sorry, I've no change but God bless, God will provide".

Another said, "Get yourself cleaned up and get a job"—as if it were that easy! To get a job I needed to be clean and tidy, no one would want to employ anyone looking the way I did. However to get clean and tidy I needed a job.

One minister took me into his house and gave me a sandwich and a cup of tea, but then asked me to sign a chit. I thought *can you spare it?* Another time I met a Methodist Minister. He took me to a run-down building saying, "You can paint this up nicely and live here". Then he told me to sign some forms that he had with him, which were incidentally, already filled in. These were so he could claim the rent money.

I've been asleep in doorways when police have dragged me out and told me to move on, but very occasionally I would meet one who was kindly disposed to people such as me. This time I was sheltering in a derelict semi-detached house with another tramp. Sometime during the night a torch shone into the house in our direction. It was a policeman looking in on us. He warned us not to stay too long as the house was due to be demolished in a couple of days. We thanked him and decided to spend one more night there before moving on. The next night the policeman was back, this time bringing some firelighters, six rashers of bacon and four slices of bread with him. He was one of the few coppers who were ever good to me. After he left, the two of us managed to find a tin, break it open and cook the bacon in it. The wonderful aroma of the sizzling bacon sharpened our appetites even more. I had pains in my stomach and couldn't wait to start eating.

We broke the rest of the firelighters up into pieces and shoved them in our pockets to keep them for another night. As the house was due for demolition the next day we collected the lead and copper piping, and left about five in the morning, taking it to the scrap yard where we exchanged it for a few *'quid'*. This was enough for a couple of pies and a cup of coffee.

I remember one time I'd been unsuccessful in scrounging a cup of tea, so I knocked on the door of a nearby house to see if they had any odd jobs that needed doing. I hoped they would offer me a cup of tea and a sandwich. I thought, *surely every human being has the right to eat at least once a day.* The door opened and before me I stood a very well-dressed woman in her mid-thirties. She was obviously very comfortably well off, so I asked her if she had any odd jobs I could do. Out of her mouth poured a cascade of abuse and bad language not befitting a lady.

"Your sorts are the lowest of the low." was one of her more polite comments. It would have been kinder if she had just said no and closed the door. I stood there speechless for a moment, knowing that I didn't deserve that kind of verbal abuse.

I thought I should let her see just how low *'people like me'* could actually go, so I went into some bushes, took off my dirty underpants, which I'd worn unwashed for the best part of a year, and later that day posted them through her letterbox! I chuckled as I thought, *well Mrs., sort them out!* It may have seemed a rash thing to do but that was unfair abuse. Over the years I've often tried to imagine the look on her face as she picked them up; they were nicely broken in.

One day, desperate for a decent meal, or indeed even a few scraps, I decided to rob a jewelers shop. I waited until it was nearly dark and no one was around, then strolled down the High Street towards the jewelers, clasping a brick tightly in my right hand. As I came within sight of the shop I took one final look around to make sure that there was no one to witness my actions, swung my arm backwards and threw the brick towards the window with all the strength I could muster. I was going to grab whatever I could through the broken window, and run for my life. Unfortunately life, dealt me a different hand. The brick hit the window with full force but instead of hearing shattering glass I felt a sharp pain on my head. I regained consciousness a few minutes later with blood trickling down my forehead. The brick had bounced off the window and knocked me out! I walked away feeling embarrassed and concussed.

Obviously this was a disaster to me at the time but in retrospect it's hilarious.

I've trekked and hitch-hiked all over Norwich, Ipswich, Newmarket, Wigan, Chorley, Blackpool, Felixstowe and many other towns besides, enduring all kinds of weather; I've eaten and drank some rubbish, and almost starved to death, but I don't blame anyone else for my downfall. Something was missing in my life. Most people would say this was common sense, but I'd suffered rejection and hurt and each time the chip on my shoulder had grown bigger. I began to wonder if it was ever going to end. I hoped each day that the next would bring about a change in my circumstances, but it didn't ... and my time was running out.

One weekend it was bitterly cold, literally freezing, and there was a deep snowfall. I was desperate and so fed up. Everything was going wrong. I thought, *I'm so cold and hungry, should I turn to crime again? I'd be better off in jail. I may as well be dead, and prison? ... I'm in prison now.* I really didn't know which way to turn. It was two o'clock in the morning and the extreme cold was fiercely biting into every part of me. My toes and fingers were in the first stages of frostbite—to this day I've trouble with them in the cold weather—and I'd been walking for hours and hours. I knew that if I stopped walking I would freeze to death.

As I trudged past house after house I noticed one in total darkness. There was a caravan in the driveway. I managed to force open the door and stepped inside. Compared to outside it was so warm in there. My cheeks and fingers were frozen. There was no food or water, but there were two sleeping bags. I unzipped one and wrapped it around me. It felt warm. I stole both the sleeping bags. I would have liked to say sorry to the owners and have paid for the damage, but how and what with? I began to walk away and soon found myself in a park. There was a shelter with a bench inside, so I lay down on it with the two sleeping bags wrapped around me. Oh, it was so warm. All I needed now was a hot drink and something to eat. I was feeling very weak and had a massive headache. In retrospect, I think that stealing those sleeping bags probably saved my life.

I stayed on the bench until about 9.30 the next morning, just lying there, unable to sleep, and daydreaming of better times ahead. When I finally managed to get up, I walked around for a while, and then wondered into the Woolworth's Store in the town centre. I pretended to be a shopper, although I don't think my awful appearance and strange odour fooled anyone. When the security guard wasn't looking I managed to steal a couple of biscuits and opened a bottle of pop and drank some. It tasted good. After 'breakfast' I just walked out.

The day grew colder with strong winds and more snow. I decided to sleep in the park shelter again. This day would be yet another day of wandering around begging whilst everyone ignored me. It was just another dreadful, miserable day. I often wondered how other tramps coped. I'm sure they managed better then me; no one should have to live like that. I so hoped the weather would change.

It did. It became brighter by day but colder at night. There was a mixture of rain, sunshine, snow and ice. Fear had truly set in, I'd all but given up hope and I knew I couldn't last much longer. I was already panicking and talking to myself much more than usual. The one thing that kept dominating my mind was knowing that nobody cared and nobody actually knew me. I was just a 'John Doe'; if I died no one would know who that dead tramp was, and my family would never find out about my death.

A couple of days slowly passed but my situation didn't improve, actually it was quite the reverse. One of my sleeping bags got wet through, so as I'd no way of drying it, I threw it away. As if that wasn't enough, my shoes split down the sides so my feet were constantly wet and cold. I even tried talking to God, (if there was one). I'd slipped into despondency

It was a Sunday night and there had been another severe drop in temperature. The snow was hard and crisp and it was getting very late. I was in my park shelter and there wasn't a soul to be seen. Except for the sound of the occasional traffic rumbling in the distance it was completely silent. From my bench I could see the house lights going out one by one. People were retiring to bed. *Lucky lot*, I thought, I didn't want to be in this situation. I desperately considered my options. Could I go to my family? Could I get back on my feet again? No it was too late for that, too much had happened. I decided I would try to sleep, but first I was going to pray. If God did exist I'd made a step in the right direction.

'Oh God', I prayed, *'I know I've made a mess of my life, but if you're out there and listening, then please answer this prayer. When I go to sleep don't let me wake up, take me to Heaven, make me warm and loved. That's all I ask, Amen.'*

I closed my eyes to sleep. For the first time ever I believed God would answer. The next morning I woke up and at first thought I must be hallucinating. I saw rabbits sleeping on my legs. My legs were lovely and warm. As I sat up the rabbits bounded off. I realised that I was still alive and began to cry, sobbing uncontrollably. You see I reasoned that either God hated me, or there was no God. This realisation helped improve my mental state. It put a spark of life back into me. I was bitter but I was going to persevere. My fighting spirit had returned.

I walked around and found two pints of milk and a small loaf on a doorstep. Now they were mine. The milk was naturally icy cold, but delicious, and the bread strengthened my ailing body.

1. Strangeways Prison, Manchester where I served three years.

2. Bedtime in the park

3. Very often I had no other choice than to search the bins for a scrap to eat.

4. It was a lonely life being a tramp. No one knew me and no one would have missed me if I had died.

5. Sometimes I slept in the bushes

6. As a tramp, I thought those warm summer days spent lying in the park with my mind blanked out with booze weren't so bad.

7. In the late 1960's the police patrolled the parks at night, and if they found a tramp they would tell them to leave. We would hide up trees, including this one, so they didn't find us and throw us out back onto the streets.

8. Andy Proctor who sang and ministered with me as Opus.

9. Today I am the manager of Freshfields Christian Music Ministries.
Left to right: Lynette Sloane, Les Deane and Chris Hall.

10. Lynette Sloane, the author of Tramps 47.

12.

Survival

I had to do something positive. A couple of weeks had passed and it was a little warmer, so I decided to wait until nightfall and go garden hopping. Maybe I would find a couple of garden sheds, have a 'mooch about' and take what I needed. I felt good in myself and was determined to survive, but had anyone tried to tell me God cared, I'd have punched them hard enough to break their nose.

My '*luck*' was changing for the better; I managed to find some Wellingtons. They were a bit big but would keep my feet dry. I also acquired some shirts and jumpers. One day I managed to beg fifteen pounds, which was much more than the total of the previous two weeks put together. With it I bought some cider, pies and biscuits, which made me feel a little stronger. After a few days I moved on and the snow disappeared. It took six or seven lifts but I managed to get to Bristol, and one generous lorry driver even gave me his sandwiches.

In my opinion, Bristol was a concrete city with every turn seeming to go uphill. The parks were excellent; they were very well maintained, and I was soon meeting other tramps and alcoholics. Unfortunately some of these poor people had completely lost their minds. Nevertheless, Bristol proved to be an excellent scrounging place, where people actually took the time to speak to you. Even the children came over for a chat, and I could get drunk every night. By now most of my drinks were mixed with 'meths'. In my position you had to drink some rubbish.

By spring, with the promise of summer just around the corner, I was able to make the most of nature's food provisions. I ate bird's eggs, wild berries and I looked forward to eating crab apples in a few months time.

* * *

Although most of this story has been about my own experiences, I've met many characters who were worse off than me. Their stories were fascinating, yet sad. Nowadays when I look back over my life I can see how God's hand was upon me, even though for a short time I classed myself as an atheist. Fortunately God knows us inside and out. There were people in the Bible who did many of the things I've done, and much worse, and God never abandoned them either.

My life on the streets was always up and down, always rough. I knew my lifestyle had been self-afflicted, but this had been compounded by people who didn't want to know, and with questions with seemingly no answers. We have four seasons and each one affects us. Sometimes kindness and love fly out of the window, self-pity climbs aboard and we only listen to ourselves.

In my later years I wrote a song reflecting upon these times:

1. The wind is blowing, the leaves are falling,

There's a change in the air and my life is passing by.

2. The world has four seasons, each one has a reason,

Oh I'm searching for the answer, the reason for my life passing by.

Summertime is so warm,

Winter is so cold,

Spring brings the changes,

And autumn the answers.

3. My life is passing me by, oh God I reach to the sky.

You're the reason I'm alive. All Your seasons are a miracle.

Oh I'm reaching out to You, I'm reaching out to You   ©

As time passed, and I became more settled in Bristol, I found myself drinking a wider variety of alcohol. 'Boozing' and lazing about had become my complete objective. I got to the stage where I was ill and would shake uncontrollably whenever I ran out of alcohol. There were still rainy days and cold nights, but I was a lot happier there.

Bristol has its fair share of churches, each one with a seemingly different message. I didn't mind that as long as no one tried to talk to me about God. Soon I found a couple of drinking partners called Dave and Ian who were complete alcoholics. We shared many a bottle of cider, and they showed me how to get cheap alcohol and where to steal it. We still usually managed to eat a few crusts every day, but never anything substantial.

Just like anywhere else, Bristol had its 'Tramps Corner' where we would all meet around an open fire at least once a week. I must admit that there were times when I still thought about leading a normal life, but there were also those warm summer nights, when I lay under the stars, the half moon shining, and my mind blanked out with 'booze'. Such times were much more enjoyable.

One day I gave my body quite a shock; I washed my face and feet, but don't worry, I didn't make a habit out if it; it had been two years since my last wash on Felixstowe beach. At this time I also noticed that there was a dangerous species hanging around the town center, St. Paul's and Staple Hill. This species was collectively known as Christians. They not only believed in God, but also had a deep practical faith. In my experience you had to be wary of such people. I figured, as long as they kept away from me they were safe. As far as I was concerned I'd found the elixir of life. It came in a bottle, blew your mind and stopped you feeling pain from outsiders, but every now and again you could still hear those annoying people singing in the town center.

Consequently this was a place I avoided at these times. I preferred the parks. Most were clean and very well kept, with a variety of plants and lots of bushes to sleep under. I could never understand how or why people could say that they found happiness in a 'so called' God, or why churches proclaimed on their huge posters that God cared.

This wasn't my experience, and most 'dossers' that I spoke to, that is, those who slept rough, would say, "Watch out for people who offer Gospel tracts telling you about Jesus, and then go away after making themselves feel good and giving themselves a reason to pray". Talk about excuses to make you feel good, I felt good when I was full of 'booze', when the sun shone, and I was warm. That was *'my kick'*. I'd tried most things in life, but nothing had worked out, so what could these people tell me about life? I refused to listen; I just cut myself off. My philosophy was *'what you see is what is real'*, although equally, there was something about them that really bothered me.

I walked to a small, very pleasant park in Staple Hill called Teewell Hill. The sun was shining and the day warm. Nearby there was a small bus station, a large row of shops, including a café, and most importantly there were pubs and off licenses. I called in at a 'rent a car' place, asking if there were any odd jobs. I was in luck, they let me wash a couple of cars, and clean up the forecourt, which earned me five pounds and a mug of tea.

It was on days like this that I felt happy, but I didn't get many days like that one. Evening arrived and by 7.30 pm. I'd made my trip to the off license and purchased a large bottle of cider and a couple of bags of crisps. Now I just had to find my bench. By this time my sleeping bag was filthy but still essential, as it kept me warm on those chilly spring nights.

I'll sit here and have a couple of swigs of cider before putting my head down for the night, I thought to myself. The visitors were leaving the park by about 9.30pm. so I was soon alone listening to the birds chattering away.

'*I won't watch telly tonight*', I joked to myself as I tried to get comfortable on my bench. Even after all this time these benches still seemed really hard!

The dawn chorus started between five and six in the morning. I have to admit that it was lovely and yet peaceful, but I was cold. I'd drunk all my cider, but still had one pound fifty left, so I planned to get a mug of coffee and toast when the café opened at nine o'clock. Now for me that wasn't a bad position to be in, although some café owners wouldn't allow tramps on their premises. You couldn't blame them for that; no one wants some smelly vagrant in their café, the customers included. While most cafés would give you a hard crust from yesterday's bread, and some might even toast and butter it for you, attitudes differed from place to place. Some people resorted to verbal abuse, others took pity. I remember one little girl giving me a biscuit. That touched me.

For some reason Bristol seemed to have better weather than anywhere else I'd been. Waves of thoughts crossed my mind about finding somewhere suitable to live, but I was dreaming again. Who was going to rent a place to someone with no money, especially if they were dirty, stinking and drunk most of the time? Instead, I decided to walk down to Fishponds Village to see if I could get some fruit and 'veg'.

There were plenty of greengrocers' shops and a market there, but I didn't get too excited because sometimes people would give and sometimes they'd shout, "Push off!"

There were already a few tramps in Fishponds. Most were alright but you always had to be on your guard against the violent tramps. They lived in fear, every crumb counted to them. I've seen them fight over a discarded bag of chips. Knowing that they could hit on good times, and then sometimes go hungry for days or weeks, they ate as much as they could, whenever they could. You had to be careful of these people. Their minds and their ability to think rationally had completely left them.

If I ate once a day I felt I'd 'done great', and it stopped me from being like those others, but it was alcohol that I needed more of. I hated the shakes and the headaches. I really didn't know how long I could go on living this way. Inside I wanted something better, and the loneliness used to get to me, especially when I saw the lights going out in the houses, as the people went to bed. How lucky they were. I just closed my eyes and hoped that I would open them in the morning.

Every day was repetitive but there was an urgency to survive. I saw people going to work, secure in their lives and not groveling around begging for food or money. I wished so much that I could be like them. How wonderful it would be to have a warm comfortable bed, to relax on a sofa and watch television, and how wonderful to use a toilet instead of 'going' behind a hedge and using leaves for toilet paper! When you are in 'your park' you see couples holding hands, kissing and cuddling and in your heart you miss this; you long for a special person to share your life. Tramps, misfits, or whatever you like to call them, are only human and have feelings, just like anyone else, but for some there is no help, some even die and most become mentally disturbed.

Well it looks like another night in Staple Hill, I thought as I made my way back through the park. *Let's hope my bench has got softer, my backside hasn't,* I teased myself.

I found a cushion that someone had thrown out—it was my first pillow for years—and I scrounged some apples and cabbage. What a mixture that meal was, but nevertheless very tasty to me. I was going to light a fire, find myself a can, fill it with water, and then mix the apple and cabbage together. Hey don't knock it, I'd had worse; I'd had nothing. *Very tasty with a capital YUK.*

13.

New Beginnings

Well they say, *good fortune is just around the corner'*, but just where was that illusive corner anyway? I'd wondered many times. Little known to me I was soon to find it.

I'd been living rough on the streets for nearly five years and had just gone through several days without a meal, and only one glass of water from a nearby household. The sun was shining and I was starving, but as no food or money was forthcoming I decided to try and sleep the day away. This was what I'd been doing lately, and feeling very sorry for myself too. I was lying down dozing on top of my sleeping bag when a young girl aged around twelve years old prodded me in the side. I opened my eyes and stared at her wondering who she was and what she wanted.

Suddenly she spouted out, "You stink ... smell awful". *Mmm*, I thought, *she's probably right*.

I said, "Go away", and off she went on her merry way. *Cheeky young madam* I thought. The sun was very warm and I soon started to nod off again. No more than five minutes later I was once more woken up by a prod to my side. *Can't a tramp get some peace?* I thought, *now what?*

I sat up, noticing the young girl with her parents and thought, *this looks like trouble,* so I asked, "Okay, What's up? Why've you disturbed me?" I just wanted to sleep.

The mother replied, "I believe my daughter insulted you."

I told her, "It doesn't matter, what she said's true."

"Well she shouldn't have been so rude to you, I'm very sorry for that", she apologised holding out her hand and giving me a pound.

Wow, I thought, *you can insult me all day and give me a pound.* To me a pound meant a meat and potato pie and a cup of tea. I thanked the kind lady who then spoke again.

"We have a spare room at home, would you be interested in staying in it?" I couldn't believe my ears. Had I met a family with no sense?

Of course I accepted, but clarified, "But I can't pay you anything".

"It doesn't matter about that". She continued, "We live in the countryside. It's quiet". *I'm in here,* I thought. I looked up towards the lady's husband. He was a tall, lean man sporting a suit. He didn't speak but seemed to be in agreement with his wife. We all walked to their car and I climbed in with them. It was a small family car, a Renault. As we drove off they all opened their windows, so we traveled all through Kingswood and Longwell Green in Bitton with a lovely breeze blowing through the car. Their vehicle came to a stop outside a very nice bungalow with extensive gardens.

Once inside I was introduced to second daughter, and a son, both in their early twenties. The family all appeared to be very close and they were definitely middle class and comfortably well off. I could imagine loads of booze coming my way, and as I looked around I noticed plenty of items that I could get a good price for down town. All I could think was how I was going to '*rip them off*'. At the same time, somewhere at the back of my mind were the thoughts, *why do they want to help me? I'm a nothing. These people are posh, what do they want with me?*

After they'd spent a few minutes showing me around their home, they took me to see my bedroom. It had a comfortable bed, a set of drawers, a wardrobe and fitted carpet. I was excited, like a kid with a new toy. Then they politely directed me towards the bathroom. Horror of horrors, the bath was full of hot soapy water. *Oh no*, I thought, quickly realising this was for me. Fear crept in. This wasn't looking good. I soon found myself in the bath, fully clothed. It was quite embarrassing too as both the husband and wife started taking my clothes off, and making sure I was *really* clean.

After my bath my long hair was cut short and my long scruffy beard was also cut, and then shaved off. I felt so clean, but yet hopeless too. I was given clean clothes, as my old ones and my sleeping bag had mysteriously disappeared, never to be seen again.

I felt so different. I discovered I had sores and scabs all over me, and I was so white. I hadn't realised that I'd lost so much weight either, more than 60 pounds in all; I was skin and bone, probably weighing no more than 120 pounds. My hair was no longer wild, but short and clean. I was in shock. It was as if my identity had been stolen from me. I felt like an alien in a strange culture. What did these people want? Why me?

Next we ate. At my request, my first proper meal was egg and chips, but surprisingly they served lettuce as an accompaniment. *How very strange*, I thought, but nevertheless, I enjoyed it all. I was told about certain house rules, and how 'The Grace' was said at every meal. *Whatever for*? I puzzled.

The food was so good, so different to the rubbish I'd been accustomed to. I wasn't used to using knives and forks or eating off clean plates either. I drank six cups of tea, and slowly realised that this family didn't want anything from me. As I sat there trying to adjust to my new surroundings I noticed little sayings about Jesus and God's love on wall plaques and pictures, and it dawned on me that this was a 'church family'. They believed in God. *Oh no*, I thought. I knew I had to make my feelings about all that '*God stuff*' quite clear to them.

"Don't preach to me!" I warned them.

"It's okay", the lady of the house replied, "God's told us to love and help you. That's all we'll do. We won't offend you, if you don't believe in God that's up to you."

The whole family was very nice and kind to me. They were definitely a very close, church run family, who believed in God, and prayed and read their Bibles everyday. As for me, I went out and got drunk. I couldn't be around or involved with all that God stuff. Let me tell you though, this was one family who went the extra mile and really cared. Every Saturday was baking day, when the family grouped up in the kitchen, and the house was filled with wonderful baking smells. *Mm*, the sweet smell of fruit pies, and the tempting aroma of steak and kidney pies were wonderful.

I was told to call the parents Mum and Dad. I suppose this was to give me some sort of family feeling, a sense of belonging. To their credit, I never heard them argue once. My first impression of Dad was of a quiet, well-dressed, old fashioned gentleman. Mum was very much the lady of the house, and definitely a lady. Dad grew all his own fruit and vegetables in the large garden. It was long, very wide, and extremely well kept. He was very '*into*' his garden, which was very productive.

During the first few months, I found it very hard to mix with the family as I felt so different. There was I, a tramp with nothing but a very large chip on his shoulder, and conversely this family who had so kindly taken me in seemed to be almost perfect. I would often say or do anything for attention, to try to cause upset or '*wind them up*'. How could they be so happy? Who or what gave them the right? They fed and clothed me and cared for me when I was ill, and yet I wanted to be unfair to them. You see, I wasn't used to being treated so well; I wasn't used to being part of a nice family, period.

Sometimes I would overhear them praying. Now this upset me. I reasoned, if God exists why does he listen to them and not to me? Here came another chip for my already crowded shoulder. *That's it*, I thought, *I'm just not good enough for God, if there is a God*. You can see how easy it is to give yourself a guilt complex, very easy indeed.

It was a strange land in which I found myself, a land where people wanted to do something for you, to change your life for the better, and give you a sense of belonging, whilst at the same time not taking anything from you in exchange. This family was giving me something that I wasn't used to having. They were a strange people indeed, and quite the opposite to the kinds of people I'd previously been involved with.

I started to ask myself more questions. *Why me? Why do they want to love and help me, and why do they really believe in God as a living person?* It seemed so far fetched, even the music they played was *'Gospelised'*. They made living look so simple. I noticed that Dad got up for work very early to have a *'quiet time'* with God, and each day when he came home he always gave his wife a kiss on the cheek.

"Had a good day dear?" she'd ask.

"Yes", he'd reply before going into the front room to read his Bible again.

"How can people live like this", I muttered to myself. "What about a drink, a cigarette, or anything I'm used to doing?" But no, they wouldn't do anything like that.

Their daughter, Sue, who was still at school, would tease me a lot, but we had lots of fun together. She was forever putting extra large wooden forks and spoons at my place at the dinner table, and then disappearing until I sat down at the table. She'd take her place with a huge grin on her face, waiting for me to notice and give my usual, *'you cheeky madam'* look. I wasn't used to getting so close to anyone, but she was a bit special. After all, it was Sue who had found me on the bench, and insulted me. She grew up to be a very clever young lady who was tops in her sport. I used to call her a Daddy's girl, as she could wrap her father round her little finger.

Dad was always working in the garden, mowing, cultivating it and planting bulbs. Once he suggested that I should find a hobby, so I thought with a chuckle, *I'll show him.* The next day when he left for work I thought, *this is it.* Later that day I collected a dozen used light bulbs, and planted them in the garden with the tops just showing.

When Dad came home the first thing I said was, "I've planted bulbs in the garden, it's my new hobby".

He smiled, saying, "Well done", and went out to look at my handy work.

"Look", I said pointing down to the bulbs and trying not to laugh.

He glanced down to where I was pointing and said, "Silly boy". Then shaking his head added, "No hope for you". As he turned away I noticed him smiling to himself.

It took me a couple of months to start getting into the family routine, but I was still drinking and when I drank I couldn't control either my mouth or temper. I was in a much better position than I could ever have hoped for, but the inner person can't be changed that easily. There were times when I thought, *any day now I'm going to be thrown back on the streets again*, but it never happened. I later learned that this family had helped other people who'd been in prison, although none of them were as bad as I'd been.

It hadn't been easy mixing with such a lovely family, but I was gradually getting used to it. With all this care they showered upon me, I'd slowly started to regain my health and was in a much-improved physical condition. My mental state was much improved too. Mum and Dad looked after me extremely well and I was very well fed, but it still puzzled me why such a family would care for me, especially as there were still days when I would drink myself silly and didn't care what I said or did.

My new family spent time together at home and regularly attended church, but I refused every invite to join them. I often heard them praying for me which still upset me. I just knew I felt empty inside and something was missing in my life, but had no idea what it could possibly be.

One evening I came home around 10.30 pm. much the worse for drink, and started shouting and knocking things over.

Mum stayed calm and simply said, "It's no use, we'll not stop loving you". *Whatever's wrong with them*, I thought. *I don't deserve such kind people.* Now another hangover awaited. For some reason God had his hand upon my life, although you couldn't have told me that at this time.

I decided to do a little work to try and earn a shilling or two. Dad loaned me his bike, a ladder, bucket and work clothes, and off I went to clean a few windows. I soon managed to get some customers, although I found the ladders heavy. On my first day I earned ten pounds, which I spent on more drink. *Not bad*, I thought.

It was very hard to come off the booze. What else was there to do anyway? My days were lonely because I found it hard to mix with others and I'd started to grow my hair long again too. It was true that I'd been offered an olive branch, a new beginning, a fresh start. I'd had my fair share of chances. My outward situation had improved almost beyond belief, but the source of my problems still lay inside. I was now really starting to wonder what this empty feeling was and why I kept trying to block it out. Who knows? Mum and Dad helped me a lot, and I knew they would always be there for me, especially when I was down, but I was in some ways like a zombie, not knowing if I was coming or going.

I signed on the dole and received a 'giro' through the post each week and Mum only took five pounds from me towards my keep. I still believe that it's a miracle that these kinds of people exist.

For a few weeks I'd been noticing that whenever I was out walking around town or visiting the pubs, I kept bumping into people giving out Gospel tracts who always told me that Jesus loved me. This would make me feel very uncomfortable and it upset me inside. Why did they seem to pick on me all the time? Why tell me about God? It was an insult.

Whenever I complained to Mum and Dad about it they would say, "Maybe God's trying to tell you something."

My reply to that was, "You live your life and believe whatever you want to, but leave me alone. Anyway what is love? As far as I am concerned it's sex. You just go with a girlfriend and sleep with each other. That's love. Then you go your separate ways and don't make a big issue of it. Sure you can like one another but forget the sloppy stuff". Why did these people have to talk about God's love, especially to me? If they wanted it they could have it. My new family said they loved me, but I couldn't understand why. Well if it made them happy, okay. I had to admit that they did like me and cared for me too. I told them a great deal about my life, such as my being in jail, but nothing I said ever put them off me. They simply kept telling me that there was better to come. I did hope so, but you could keep this love thing out of it. I couldn't cope with that side of life.

Early one warm sunny day I decided to go into Bristol Town Center to share some cider with some street people. At least we would have something in common. I sat on a wall and shared my bottle with a tramp called Alf. What a character he was. Suddenly, out of the blue a young lady walked up to me, put a Gospel tract in my hand, and started speaking to me. I looked up at her and it struck me how pretty she was.

"Jesus loves you". She said. Instantly I felt anger rising up inside me. I was furious and upset too.

"Can't I just sit down and share a bottle with a mate without this intrusion?" I asked her raising my voice. I glanced down at the tract. "What? Jesus again!"

I screwed it up, grabbed the girl and pushed it in her mouth; snapping at her, "Keep away from me with your tracts! Tell your leader I'm not interested." I saw tears and fear in the girl's eyes. Now I felt awful so I told her, "You shouldn't have come near me, I'm no good. The Church is for good people, not low life like me".

Drawing a little courage from somewhere she replied, "Yes but God loves you too. The Bible says 'All have sinned, no one's perfect'." I got up and walked away feeling pretty awful. You just don't need that intrusion when you are out trying to enjoy a quiet drink and mixing with your own kind. You see, I found it very hard to get to another level of life because if I tried to look deeper into myself or felt threatened or I would always go back to the booze. It was my refuge.

I decided to spend the rest of the day in Bristol, and then to slowly walk the nine miles home at about two or three in the morning. This way everyone would be in bed asleep and no one would bother me.

On my way home I had to walk down a lane in Longwell Green that had no streetlights. There was a new moon so it was very dark. I could hear voices coming from the other side of the road, but couldn't see anyone. I'd walked that way home many times but had never encountered anyone else out there at that time of night before.

As the voices got closer I could just about make out that they belonged to three ladies walking towards me. The ladies were laughing and clearly enjoying themselves, so I thought they must have been returning home from a party. How wrong could I've been?

I was half drunk and shouted, "Goodnight ladies".

One of the ladies shouted back, "Goodnight and God bless." As they passed one of them came over and handed me a Gospel tract.

"Read that in the morning" she said, and added, "Jesus loves you". I walked on, fuming. What was going on, people telling me 'Jesus loves you', even at that time in the morning? My night was completely spoilt. Later I found out that they had been on their way back from a prayer meeting.

I arrived home. There was a note for me on the table. 'Goodnight' it read.

I shouted out loud, "If only I could have a good night! No chance tonight."

I woke up the next day wondering if the events of the previous twenty four hours had really taken place. What was going on? It was all so frustrating. I arose, got washed, dressed and ate breakfast. I told Mum about the previous day.

"Maybe God's trying to speak to you" she remarked. I wanted to scream but controlled myself. I just sat there quietly thinking, *why do they talk like that? What's wrong with them? Life is life.* My head was muddled. These people were good and kind and I didn't want to insult them but couldn't they see I was a waster?

Sunday morning came and Mum and Dad were preparing to go to church as usual. This meant I could have a root around the house to see what I could find; after all I was getting short of money. Suddenly, while they were still getting ready to go out, a brown envelope dropped through the letterbox. I picked it up casually mentioning that there was no name on it.

Mum said, "Open it up, it's probably advertisements". I tore it open and pulled out some leaflets. One said, 'Welcome'. It was from a new Elim Pentecostal Church, which had opened up in Keynsham. 'A Warm welcome awaits, God loves you and you are invited'. I blew my top!

"Look", I said, "There's no escape. They even shove it through your door! Who are these people?"

Mum laughed. "Oh dear", she said. "Maybe you should go there. You can tell them not to send you any more tracts". If I was going to go to this new church it would be to punch the Pastor on his nose. What an invasion of privacy that was, fancy posting Gospel News through someone's letterbox. These Gospel tracts were beginning to haunt me, and these Christians who kept informing me that God loved me were really annoying me. I didn't even believe in God. Frustration and panic were building up inside me. However, I did as Mum suggested and went down to the Keynsham church.

I stood outside the freshly renovated, red brick building for a moment. There was a notice board in front, with a poster on it which grabbed my attention. This added to the insult. It read, 'Welcome, you have arrived at the right place'. Now I was livid. *How dare they say that?* I thought, taking it as a personal insult to myself.

I walked into the church. It seemed to be empty, but then I heard noises coming from a room at the rear of the building, so I went to investigate. I opened the door, and stepped inside. At the back of the room I saw a few elderly folk praying. They were asking God to bring people to the meeting that evening.

As I stood there I felt something come over me. It was a feeling I'd never encountered before. My anger had gone and been replaced with something else. I just didn't know what that something else was. I became aware of tears running down my cheeks. I turned and left the room without a word.

As I bid my hasty retreat I looked up and noticed an inscription on the wall behind the preachers stand. It read, 'With loving kindness have I drawn thee unto me'. This was like an arrow piercing my heart. *What is this?* I asked myself, *what's going on?* I turned around and left the church with mixed feelings. When I got home I sat in my bedroom pondering the morning's events. I couldn't understand how walking into a church could have such an effect on me.

Later on I spoke to Mum and Dad whilst trying to hide my feelings. Mum suggested that I should go to the 6.15 pm. meeting to see what was going on. I reasoned, well it'll be all right, after all it can't affect me; I'm tough. As I was still thinking along these lines, Mum's elderly mother, whom I'd been told to call Grandma, asked if I would take her to the meeting. I agreed.

Just before we set off the old lady said, "Wait, God's told me to wear a green coat; someone else will also be wearing a green one, and I've to pray for her." I thought, *madness. How can this be right?*

We set off. Grandma, now in her green coat, was very happy.

She said, "Well my son, you're in for a new experience."

I laughed, "You don't want to believe in all that Gospel stuff." As we approached the church I started feeling nervous, and that funny feeling began to return. I thought, *maybe I shouldn't go in*, but as I had helped Grandma out of the car and up the pathway, it felt natural to walk into the church together. I was amazed at there being so many young people there, all cheerful and singing like they were actually enjoying themselves. Tambourines and guitars were being played. This seemed strange to me, not my idea of church at all; I thought people were supposed to look miserable, and that someone would be thumping out a dirge on an old tuneless organ.

At 6.30 pm the meeting started. Two of the choruses they sang were, 'I've got joy bells in my heart' and 'In my heart there rings a melody'. It struck me that the people sang as if they felt and meant every word. After the singing stopped the preacher stood up and told everyone to move from their seats and greet everyone else. I noticed a lady in a green coat as Grandma predicted. Grandma went straight over and started praying for her. Now I was worried. A few minutes later we all sat down.

The Pastor walked over to the centre of the stage and greeted us all in Jesus' name.

"Let God speak to your heart" he said. Then he began to preach. As he spoke I noticed an aura of light surrounding him, which I attributed to background lighting, although afterwards I found out that there were no background lights. All the time he spoke it seemed as if he was preaching directly to me, telling me of God's love, how empty I was and how Jesus had suffered for me. Tears ran down my face. I could feel love entering my being. I tried to fight it, refusing to believe what was happening, but as the preacher spoke I was breaking down. It was as if Jesus was standing in front of me asking me to accept what he'd done for me, personally. I felt so warm ... and tingly, although words cannot adequately describe the experience. The Pastor asked for anyone who had felt touched by the service to go to the front, and I felt strangely urged to do so. So I did, and there I accepted Jesus as my Saviour.

It was as if a huge sack of coal, a great weight, had lifted off my back. I felt so light. My sins, my blindness, and my emptiness had all vanished. God had started a work in my life. Instead of emptiness I felt joy, and happiness. I felt free. I had the joy bells they'd been singing about in *my* heart. I was a new creation. I felt all new inside. I saw how God had kept his hand on me all those years, keeping me alive to hear the Gospel. I was a sinner washed and saved by grace (God's love and favour), although for my part it was totally undeserved.

Lost in the realisation of God's love and forgiveness, I felt so different, and then it occurred to me that I had to go home and tell Mum and Dad what had happened. One part of me was feeling elated, but the whole idea of me going to church that evening was to show churchgoers that church wasn't anything special. Pride kicked in. I decided that on my return home I would go straight to my bedroom and so avoid having to tell anyone about my experience. But it was fantastic; I'd never felt so loved. In the space of a few minutes

God had changed my life; filling it with so much joy I couldn't stop laughing. I was on a high and that empty feeling I'd experienced all my life had gone!

I drove home with Grandma and helped her to the front door. Now this was the point at which I had to walk straight through the living room, and pretend that nothing had happened. As I made my way through the house Mum and Dad noticed straight away that something *had* happened to me.

Mum took one look at me and exclaimed, "Les, your face looks all alive and your eyes are sparkling." I went to the bathroom without replying and checked in the mirror. It was true I could see new life in my eyes and whole face. There was no other way to describe it.

On return to the living room I told the whole family what had happened and how God had spoken into my life. They were elated. That night a work had started in me. The Bible says that, 'I am a new creation' (2 Corinthians 5 v 17); I am Born Again, in God's eyes spiritually a little child. Jesus went to the cross for me.

With his outstretched arms he said, 'This is how much I love you, and I'll never, never leave you nor forsake you'. God has kept that promise no matter what has confronted me since, and I shall never forget his word before I was saved, 'With loving kindness have I drawn thee unto me'. (Jeremiah 31 v 3) How true these words are and he has kept his word to me. Now I couldn't wait to see what future lay ahead.

14.

The Potter and the clay

Writing this book has not been easy. There have been so many confrontations, so many memories, good and bad, but in this world of ours, no matter what our situation, God really cares for us, his creation. I've come to realise what a sad person I'd been, having had the chance of great material wealth, and yet in the end choosing the life of a tramp. When I had money I had friends, yet a few short years later, living on the streets, no one knew me; I was just another John Doe.

During my former gang days times were affluent. This was when I bought my first home.

This particular day, as I walked around Ipswich town I noticed a new exclusive housing estate. Some of the houses were complete but others were still under construction.

I'd like to live in one of those houses I thought to myself, so I walked into the sales booth and addressed the smartly attired salesman, "Ow much mate?" He looked up from his desk, a little surprised to see before him a young man wearing a denim jacket, tea shirt and scruffy jeans. His clientele would normally have been very middle class and tastefully dressed.

"Eight thousand for that one" he answered pointing to the viewing house. What a lovely home it was: stylish, airy and light with a beautifully designed kitchen and comfortable living room. Later that day I went back to see one of the finished houses.

Being eager to get a sale, the salesman tried to explain how to get a mortgage, but I didn't let him finish.

"A mortgage? I don't need a mortgage" I said reaching into my jeans pocket and pulling out a load of cash.

"Oh" he replied looking a little shocked. I handed him eight thousand pounds bundled up into rolls of a thousand pounds in each.

Within a few days the house was mine and ironically, when it was time for me to move on I sold it to a policeman.

That was long before, during the ensuing years, I alienated my family and caused many others to turn against me, while all the time the answer was in Jesus. Fulfillment is found in him. In this respect there is nothing wrong in wealth, nothing wrong in being poor. The joy of the Lord can be found in both.

I'd walked on both sides of the law, lost out on both sides, and had struggled to find love and peace. In prison I found fear, violence, and humiliation and witnessed others breakdown mentally. When I first went into prison I remember the governor telling me I'd given up the right to be treated as a human being. I was a number, a 'go for'. I no longer had the right to have any say in how I lived. I'd stripped myself of being part of humanity. In turning to crime I'd been searching for the things in life that most people have to work hard for.

Now God had opened my eyes. He had set me free. I remember a song, 'My chains fell off' and how true these words are. Jesus didn't give me a number, he wrote my name in the Lamb's Book of Life.

As a young Christian God had so much to do in my life, this was truly a new beginning. I had so many hang ups and hurts that I knew God would heal. Through writing down and sharing my experiences, I hope to show others who have gone through, or who are still going down the road of similar experiences, that the victor is Jesus. The answer is Jesus, and there is help for everyone who wants it, for God says, 'I'll never, never forsake you'. (Hebrews 13 v 5)

When I became a Christian I thought that things would change for the better. However, becoming a Christian doesn't miraculously turn life into a bed of roses. A work had begun in me, but I still drank, gambled and had worldly desires. True, I'd taken that first step, but I'd no idea what would happen next, or what was expected of me.

In the beginning I felt as if I were floating on air most of the time, but at other times I came down to earth with a bump. It all needed a lot of explaining to me. For instance, what had happened at my conversion, and how was Jesus going to make a new person out of me?   I wondered if I would be expected to change straight away. I hoped not. Frustration began to set in until a young couple from church, Julian and Glenys, came around to the house to see how I was getting on.

They were doing what is called 'a follow up' on new Christians, that is, seeing how they're getting on and what help they might need. These two people became a blessing to me and their influence was an enormous help. We were able to talk at length about my past and future, and they often picked me up in their car and drove me to church meetings.

At this early stage in my Christian walk it was crucial to be '*fed*' the right spiritual food, with no hang-ups. I found praise and worship particularly fascinating. Attending Bible Studies and prayer meetings showed me how other people spoke to the Living God, and I witnessed how God works so diversely in so many different lives.   We are all individuals to him, coming from wide-ranging backgrounds and cultures, and having such varied lives.

Although I still drank a lot, I didn't feel condemned. Instead I was told that I was the clay and God was the potter, and he'd mould, shape and change me. In his eyes I was already perfect.

A few weeks later a friend asked me to go to a special healing meeting at City Temple, Elim Pentecostal Church in St. Paul's, Bristol to see God's anointing on those who needed prayer. I saw God move in that place. I saw people going forward for prayer, and the minister and church elders laying hands on them, and I heard them praising God for what He had done in their lives. All this was so new and exciting to me. I just wanted more; I was hungry for God that night, and at the end of that meeting came away spiritually very well fed.

My time living on the streets had left me with a real drink problem, and since becoming a Christian this had become a constant fight within me. I knew that I shouldn't be drinking and really wanted to give it up, but at the same time realized I couldn't do it by myself. I'd been drinking too much for too long to give up just like that, so I kept drinking. I really needed medical help. The Devil tries to use your weakness, but God uses whatever you give him, including your weaknesses, and turns them into his opportunities. He'll turn your weakness into your testimony, if you let him. At this stage I felt inadequate as a Christian, but deep inside I knew God understood, so I decided to go to a drying out clinic.

I didn't have an easy time at the clinic but the people who ran it were very understanding. I felt emotionally low all the time, very unwell and was hallucinating wildly. Everything around me looked many times larger than reality. A giant fly, bigger than my head, was continually buzzing around and wouldn't leave me alone. I had buzzing noises in my head anyway regardless of that stupid fly. The bath was massive and looked like a swimming pool which, in my emotionally unstable state, scared me as I couldn't swim. I thought I would drown. The meals were massive too. At any other time giant-sized dinners would have seemed great, but right now I didn't feel at all like eating, and the teaspoon appeared to be the size of a spade. I wondered how it would ever fit in my mouth.

For the first three days I was in excruciating pain. My head was pounding and I could feel my stomach tightening. My lips were blue, swollen and so dry. My tongue was dry too, and my eyes were bulging. The nurses must have been used to witnessing this, but I was shocked. In my opinion I looked like I'd spent night after night '*on the booze*' rather than in trying to come off it!

If there was ever a time when I thought I was cracking up, this was it. Over those few days I cried in despair many times because I just wanted to get out of there, and get as far away as possible. There wasn't anything to hold me at the clinic—no locked doors or windows—I could have walked out at any time, but I was determined to get over this hurdle, so I cried out to God, and he gave me the strength and grace to get through the crisis, and gain the victory.

We come to many rocky places in life when we can so easily turn and run away, but if we do we just come up against that same problem again later on. Sometimes God doesn't simply take the problem away, but He gives us the strength to 'go through it' and in doing so we grow a little more and gain that victory.

I was only at the clinic for a week, but it seemed an eternity. When I left to go home I'd been off the booze for seven whole days, but still felt ill. I was glad to be home and reading my Bible, but my drinking problem wasn't completely over yet. I'd prayed for help and other Christians had talked with me about it, but I still felt that I needed further professional help.

On the following Sunday I decided to go to church and see if the Pastor would pray for me. I chose to travel by bus which was a big mistake. I was still feeling emotionally very low, and physically weak. When I arrived at the bus stop, two lads in their late teens were already waiting for the bus. They stared at me, noticing my Bible.

"Why you 'olding a Bible?" the first one asked.

"I'm on my way to church." I answered. They laughed sarcastically. I started to feel angry, adding, "Push off, I'm not in the mood for bother". Continuing to laugh the second teenager spat in my face. I lost my temper and grabbed the nearest lad, roughly pushing him to the floor and holding him there. Inside I wanted to cry, I felt so feeble. My Bible was still in my other hand, so I placed it on the floor and punched the lad in the face. Then, leaving my Bible behind, I turned and walked away in shock, my mind racing, thinking, *I'm supposed to be a Christian!*

The Devil had a right go at me. I headed straight to a pub, got very drunk and started a fight. What a night. I left the pub feeling really awful, thinking I'd blown it with my new faith.

Staggering to a nearby phone box, I managed to phone a Christian friend who came out and took me home in his car. I apprehensively explained the evening's events to Mum and Dad. They were not at all condemning. Instead they comforted me, explaining that although it can be rough at times, I must learn not to turn to violence or alcohol, but call on God instead; He'd be there for me. That night I felt so low; I knew then that the Christian life wasn't going to be easy. I had to learn to trust the Lord; on my own I was weak. I sensed the Lord speaking to my heart, "I shall never leave you", (Hebrews 13 v 5), and God never has let me down, neither at that time nor to the present day. Right then I decided to trust God to stop me from drinking and smoking. In *His* strength I was going to see the victory.

One day soon afterwards I went to the pub. The barman passed me my pint of beer. It tasted awful so I got a replacement. This tasted awful too so I ordered a whisky. I took a sip.

"Ugh", I spluttered, "That's disgusting". The barman politely assured me that his beer and whisky were 'okay'. I tried another pub but it was the same story there, it all tasted awful. I knew my prayers had been answered; my drinking days were over.

I sought God even more and wouldn't miss a church service. It was at this time that I heard something quite unknown to me; people were praying in a foreign language. I asked the Pastor about it and he told me that it was the Baptism in the Holy Spirit. He explained that it was a language that God gives to believers to pray to him. I knew I wanted this. I hungered for more of God, wanting to be like His Son.

The Pastor laid hands on me and prayed that I would receive the Holy Spirit. Nothing happened. I didn't feel any different. *Maybe it's not for me*, I thought; *I'm not good enough.*

The following week I visited a church called The Mount of Olives where there was a guest speaker called Don O' Don. During the course of the meeting he asked those who wanted prayer for the Baptism in the Holy Spirit to come forward. Five people made their way to the front, and I followed making it six. He laid hands on us all, praying for us. The other five were filled with the Holy Spirit and started singing in tongues. Some were crying with joy as well. As for me, I didn't get anything. I felt so left out. I thanked God for my salvation and his love, but I wanted more. I wasn't feeling bad but I really wanted what they received.

As I walked by that same church the following night I saw a sign outside announcing that Don O' Don was there again, this time with Don Double. I didn't known about this second meeting, but strolled in.

The meeting was nearly over and I took my seat just as Don Double finished speaking. He looked up in my direction and then walked right up to me.

Laying hands on my head he said, "Receive your blessing". I spoke, or rather, cried out in tongues. What a beautiful feeling, my whole body shook. *At last*, I thought, *Praise God.*

Considering my background and the life I'd led previous to my conversion, this was a complete turn around.

I just couldn't figure out how God could look at someone like me and say, "I love you with an everlasting love". God hadn't only given me his salvation but had turned my life upside down. The Christian life wasn't an easy option, but knowing that I had a Saviour to turn to in every situation was wonderful. This still means everything to me. This is what had been missing from my life.

Two years passed and 1983 dawned. Even though I'd been saved and baptised in the Holy Spirit for a while, I still had many things in my life which needed sorting out. There were hurts, emotional scars and fear still to be dealt with. Only God could do this. I was going to be open to allowing the Potter to mould and make me. After all, He is the Creator.

I still had to learn how to communicate with others and to love and trust them. All this was alien to me. After one particular meeting everyone in the church went to shake hands and give each other a hug.

I wasn't used to this kind of friendliness, so when a Christian Brother came up to me, shaking my hand and trying to put his arms around me, I objected saying, "Whoa, Steady on, I'm not gay". Then, when a young lady came over to me and gave me a hug and a kiss on the cheek I thought she fancied me. How wrong I was. The Pastor explained that people do this as a demonstration of God's love for each other. *Very strange*, I thought. I had to pray that God would open my eyes to this sort of love and friendship. I soon learned how God builds his church on love and devotion; after all, his love and devotion were shown to us when his Son died on that cross. What love God has, how deep!

I've always had a great sense of humour, and becoming a Christian hadn't diminished it. I loved practical jokes. Now, many people living in the countryside bordering Bristol grow their own vegetables. My next door neighbour was a famous evangelist and he grew massive cabbages. One Sunday afternoon this neighbour was in his garden having a quiet word with God, as was his custom. I was hiding in his cabbages, waiting to have some fun with him.

As he lowered his head and started to pray silently I began shaking the large cabbage leaves and cried out, "Melvin, this is the lord your cabbage. You are to preach tonight". I was still hiding and so didn't see him reaching a bucket of water. A few seconds later I was drenched to the skin as the icy cold water landed all over me and the cabbages. He knew who it was.

"Les" he shouted, trying not to laugh, "One day you are going to preach and my turn will come". Even preachers can have a laugh.

For a while I'd been praying for a job, and now was the time the Lord chose to open up such a door of opportunity. I heard of a job in a wood preservation warehouse and went along for an interview. The job description was simply 'filling barrels with creosote and wood preserver'. When I arrived there were six other men, about twice my size, also applying for the job. Even the barrels were bigger than me. It was time for a prayer. My name was called and I entered the office. The boss asked me what I could offer.

"A good days work", I replied, "And a willingness to learn".

"Okay", the boss said, "You start tomorrow". *Wow*, I thought, *an answer to prayer, Alleluia.*

I found the work very hard going but was told I showed promise. Each day I prayed before I left for work, and thanked God on my return home. I soon managed to tell my workmates about Jesus and God's love, and so the Gospel reached into that place. My friends Julian and Glenys still came around most nights and regularly took me to evening meetings. I was so fortunate that this couple had taken such an interest in helping me. Mum and Dad were very happy with my progress and the whole family had been surprised at the change in me.

About seven weeks later I had a bit of an accident at work. I was in a hurry and lifted a barrel incorrectly. Red hot pain seared through my back. I knew the correct way to lift so this was really infuriating. I was sent home in a lot of pain.

Slowly, I lowered myself and edged onto a kitchen chair. I didn't know hurting my back would be so painful. After a few minutes in this position the pain eased a little. The next problem was trying to get up. It took a couple of minutes to manoeuvre myself to the edge of the chair and then push myself up with my arms while trying to straighten my back. How foolish I'd been to lift that barrel that way. The doctor came out and told me to have a couple of weeks off work. The pain was terrible, so it was back to prayer for me. At 6.45 that evening the Pastor came to see me. He was on his way to a new church in Bath, and taking one look at me agonizing in the chair, told me he was taking me with him. I imagined how difficult it would be getting in and out of the car, but knew inside that I needed to go.

As soon as we entered the church I noticed the fantastic atmosphere. The Pastor took a seat in the front row and I very gingerly sat down next him. Whilst we were all singing choruses and praising God everything suddenly became quiet. The Pastor began to pray for everyone and then came down and prayed over me. My back pain disappeared. I was able to jump for joy. God had healed me. I'd received my miracle. What a mighty God!

15.

My Genetic Family and God

There were lots of ups and downs in my early Christian life. Some experiences were good and some I didn't enjoy quite as much. God was dealing with me; I needed turning inside out. The Bible says that when you get saved 'all things become new, your old life passes away and you become a new creation' (2 Corinthians 5 v 17), but as with any baby or young child, there can be teething problems. Balancing my new life wasn't going to be easy, as I was finding out.

Although my back was healed, I took my time off work as an opportunity to go home to Manchester and tell my whole family I'd become a Christian.

"I've given my life to Jesus" I told them. Well that didn't go down too well. They didn't understand, but I managed to witness to them all and hoped the Holy Spirit would show them what had happened in my life.

One of them said, "Oh no, he's going to rob churches now". They do say that the hardest people to witness to are the members of your own family, I suppose because they know us so well and know all our faults. I had to leave it with them. Hopefully they would notice a change in my lifestyle and character. You see, we have to live out our Christian life and not just talk about it. People need to see Jesus in us, in the way we live, talk and react, not just in what we tell them.

I visited many of my Aunts and Uncles and told them how God had changed my life. Some listened to what I had to tell them, but others weren't even bothered. I could understand that; I'd been notorious within the family. My life wasn't good until I met the Lord. It's still very much on my heart how much God could speak to this entire world if they would only listen. These precious words of scripture declare, 'For God so loved the world', (John 3 v 16) –yes, he really does love every one of us.

I returned to Bristol, to my newfound family, and back to work. I was thinking to myself, *Jesus is Lord and I'll see my real parents saved. There is Heaven and there is Hell. I want my family in Heaven.* What the future held I didn't know.

After a few weeks I received a distressing phone call. My natural father had suffered a heart attack. I returned to Manchester to see him and had the chance to lead him to Jesus. He accepted Jesus as his personal Saviour. I still praise God for that. Soon afterwards he suffered another heart attack and died. What a shock this was for the whole family and so sad for my Mum. She and Dad had spent a lifetime together, raising eleven children, through good times and hard times … and now he was gone.

A couple of months passed by and this time it was my Mum I had to visit in hospital. She had cancer and tuberculosis and had already had a lung removed. I stood by her bed looking down at her. She looked so small, weak and fragile, and weighed no more than seventy pounds. I was very upset; it broke my heart to see her like that. I prayed so hard for her and God heard my requests; my prayers were answered. While I was at her bedside she gave her life to Jesus, right there in that hospital. Two days later I visited her again and this time she was sitting up in bed. I cracked some jokes and did a few impressions for her. Mum laughed the way she always did and told me she'd had a dream, which seemed more like a vision.

In it, Saint Peter was standing at the gates of Heaven and he spoke to her: "May", which was her name, "Don't worry, there is joy and a beautiful place here for you".

Mum said to me, "Les don't worry, I'm okay". With that I left. When I arrived home I told my sisters and brothers that Mum was all right, but my older sister, Pam informed me that the hospital had just phoned. Mum had passed away. I could neither believe nor understand it. She had seemed so much better. As we shared our grief I felt God send the comforter to us all, and I shed tears of joy as well as sadness that night. I knew Mum was safe, I knew where she had gone.

16.

My Inner Hurts

After Mum's funeral I returned again to Bristol. What a difference there had been in my life since I'd accepted Jesus. Equally, I still had a lot of hurt and invisible scars that needed to be dealt with. A friend asked me if I would like to go to an inner healing meeting. Now some people do not believe in inner healing. They say that when you get saved God takes all your hurts, and fears away straight away, but what about any hurts we receive during the years after we come to him? These need healing too. I knew I still had inner hurts. He hadn't taken all mine away yet. Up until now I'd never heard of inner healing, but I went along and saw God bring healing into many people's lives.

A lady, a complete stranger, walked over to me and prayed a prayer of intercession. God revealed to her how hurt and bitter I'd been and how he was going to deliver me, making me rise up like the eagle. I just wept as I confessed my bitterness and God took it all away. In exchange he poured his love into me. It was like a cleansing. I felt wonderfully released. To quote a lady I admire very much, 'Jesus really does heal you everywhere you hurt!'

The people in the group worshipped and praised God. It was an experience that is really hard to adequately explain, but consider this, the thief who became a tramp and turned against God, was now here in a Christian meeting, forgiven, healed and praising God with his whole heart! What a mighty God; He can take a broken life and so completely change it around.

Today my life as a Christian is still not perfect. I do still sometimes get things wrong and can make mistakes. Occasionally my mouth runs away with me, and most times I run when I should walk, but the wonderful truth is that God is always there to pick me up and show me my mistakes. He always allows us room to be human and never condemns us for it.

Back in Bristol, I was very surprised to find out that my new family didn't believe in baptism by total immersion. Here was a family of dedicated Christians, baptised in the Holy Spirit, and yet not baptised in water, and until now they had never spoken to me about it. At church that Sunday evening the Pastor announced that there would be a baptismal service in two weeks time. The candidates would be totally immersed in water, and those who wanted to be baptised were to let the Pastor know. *Well*, I thought, *it's time I got baptised in water*, so I put my name down. Mum and Dad were pleased and told me the family would be there. I asked my elder brother David to come up from Manchester too.

The big day arrived and the baptismal service started. After the praise and worship and a short bible reading, the seven other candidates and myself walked forward to the baptistery, all dressed in white. It was a wonderful service and God's blessing was on everyone. One after the other, each candidate stepped into the water, gave testimony to how Jesus had changed their lives, and were baptized. Last of all came my turn. As I stepped down into the tank and the water rose up to my chest, I gave testimony of God's undeserved love and favour in my life. David wasn't saved but tears ran down his face. God spoke into his life. As I was baptised I felt the Holy Spirit rest upon me. It was so beautiful. After I climbed out of the baptismal tank the Pastor asked if anyone else wanted to follow through the waters of baptism.

My new family stood up and said, "Yes, we do". *Praise God*, I thought. They all got baptised in water that night. What a blessing God poured on that family. A mighty work had started in them. They were all so excited about God.

'It's no secret what God can do. What he's done for others he'll do for you'. Christians can sing this song with truth. It's a serious time in anyone's life when they feel that the world is against them, that there is no one who listens or understands; suicide is on the cards and with no one to turn to depression is top of the list. A cry for help often just echoes passed deaf ears, yet if we cry out to God he'll surely answer. Even King David, living all those years ago in Bible times, came to a place in his life when he cried out, 'Hear my cry, oh Lord ... from the depths of my heart do I cry to You'

I know now that God heard *my* cry to him all that time ago when I lay shivering on my park bench on that freezing cold night. Back then I really believed that if God was real He would take me and I wouldn't wake up. When I awoke the next morning to find myself still alive, I was so disappointed that I wept. I thought that there was no God, and so there was no hope, but He did answer that desperate cry to him. I've cried out to Him since being saved too, when I've got things wrong. Then when I've fallen God has picked me up, even though the Devil has tried to convince me I was a fool.

At such times I just remember my salvation, how God came into my life, and I know the truth. I've probably upset a few Pastors in my time, thinking or even knowing I know more than some of them, but how often do our own children come home and tell us that they know what is best for them, young and inexperienced as they are. You see, at the time we are saved we can be likened to little children, first of all being brought up on milk, which is the Gospel and then progressing onto meat, that is, to maturity in the word. We always want more than our parents and seek the best. We can get greedy, jealous, and over zealous, but then comes the time when we start to grow up and mature in our relationship with God. God reveals himself to us more and more, and blesses and disciplines us. Such is his love.

After a while of continuing in the Christian walk, and seeing God's gifts manifest in the church, I got a hunger to receive a gift of the Spirit myself. I loved praying in tongues. (It's such a beautiful way of connecting with God through the Holy Spirit). I also heard people sing in tongues. What a holy, beautiful sound. I'd heard the gift of prophesy to the church too and wanted to be part of all that. I sought God to bless me with these gifts. It was God's fulfillment that I wanted. I wanted to serve Almighty God.

17.

Each day New and Exciting

As I wrote this book I hoped that each page would say something different to the reader. To me every day with Jesus is different and exciting. Sometimes Christians will be on top of the mountain so to speak, whilst at other times down in the valley as the Prophets often were, but each day God teaches us something new. We only have to be open to him and have a willingness to learn. God has given us hope and grace, which is his undeserved love, favour and enabling.

In the world we say, "I hope it doesn't rain", or, "I hope everything will be alright", but this hope is never a certainty. It's only a maybe; there is room for doubt. Biblical hope is always the expectation of something good, and Jesus is the object of the believer's hope. Therefore Biblical hope is the opposite of worldly hope. It's not a maybe but a 'will be'. We truly can say with confidence, 'My hope is in The Lord!' (Psalm 39 v 7) Before Jesus set me free I was in slavery to sin. It ruled my life but now I am free to praise my God.

I'd been asking God to use me in the gifts for a while but nothing had happened. Far from getting despondent I just carried on as normal knowing that God's timing was, and is, always perfect. One Sunday evening a visiting evangelist,

Melvin Banks spoke at our church. It was filled to capacity, every seat taken. The hymn singing was wonderful and the message and testimonies were fantastic.

At the conclusion of the meeting there was an alter call. The speaker asked for anyone who wanted to be saved, or to have prayer for healing, to come forward to the front of the church where he'd minister to them all. The people streamed forward expectantly. After this time of ministry the Pastor announced that the meeting was closing with a prayer. For a moment it became silent, then suddenly I felt the Holy Spirit come upon me and I gave a message in tongues. This was the first time God had used me in this way. The evangelist gave the interpretation. What a miracle; what a blessing. To say that I was on fire for God that night was an understatement. After the meeting closed people were still rejoicing. As soon as I walked into the living room back home Mum commentated on what a bright face I had, so I told her of the blessing I'd received at church.

I've found that Jesus is the answer to all the bad times and experiences I've been through in life, and there many more that I've not even mentioned. In fact, He is the answer to all the worlds' problems. The Bible tells us that 'If a man says there is no God he is a fool'. (Psalm 14 v 1) In view of all that is happening in our world today—the suffering, lost and confused people not knowing which way to turn—now is the time to stop being a fool and turn to God. My testimony only proves what God did for me, but God tells us that all who call on him through Jesus shall find life.

Nowadays I often think of the people who still live on the streets—the tramps and dropouts trying to escape whatever brought them to their decision to live rough—and the reasons why they choose such a down-trodden life. I remember those bitterly cold nights, and those warm, sunny yet empty days, and I've often gone back to try and seek out some of the people who helped me during my days as a tramp, but I've never been able to find any of them.

Occasionally the newspapers have told of a person found dead from exhaustion and the cold, maybe they were found on a park bench. One tramp jumped into the canal. He couldn't take that life anymore. This is how hard street living gets. There is a lovely chorus we sing. 'Jesus take me as I am; make me whiter than the snow'. It's the believer's responsibility to minister the Gospel to all and this thought should be on our minds. We need to reach these people because Jesus loves them, and He loves them just the way they are. No one should ever think of them as worthless rubbish, because God puts such a high value on their lives—the death of His Son, Jesus. I am so fortunate that God chose me and keeps his hand upon my life and has used me to counsel and minister to many down and outs and people whose lives are depressed. God bless them.

One day my friend, Tommy and I were strolling by a riverbank in Preston and talking about how our lives had changed since being saved. It was warm and dry and the sun had lifted our spirits. As we continued on our way we noticed a young woman of about twenty walking towards us holding a kitten. Not seeming to notice us at all, suddenly, just a few yards ahead of us, she threw herself and the kitten into the river. Without thinking Tommy and I jumped in after her to pull her out. Fortunately it wasn't deep; the waters only came up to my waist. I was thankful for this because as I mentioned earlier, I can't swim. We helped the girl and her kitten safely onto the riverbank. My heart was pounding as I am sure theirs were. I hadn't known how deep the river was as the waters were murky. We could all have drowned. We spoke to the girl, Tommy nursing the frightened, wet kitten.

"Why did you do that?" I asked.

"I'm fed up" she replied. "My life's hopeless". We took her and her kitten to the local police station where they got a social worker. The police gave Tommy and me a hot drink and a warm blanket before giving us a lift home.

I grounded myself in the Word of God, attended Bible College, and studied very hard. God gave me a great understanding of His word. This part of my Christian life wasn't a big problem for me. I know that sometimes young Christians may not find it as easy to understand the Bible, but in my case it was my normal walk of life where I was a little unstable, though I never left my faith behind. I was learning about relationships between men and women, and how to treat each other with respect. The love God blessed me with allowed me to reach others. My desire was to serve Him in truth with my whole heart.

* * *

Time passed. I was in my mid forties, had been saved for about twelve years and had just come through another very low time in my Christian life. Sometimes it's hard to pick yourself up when you are feeling very low, but as I've mentioned many times, God never leaves you.

Another friend, Chris introduced me to Pastor John Young who was pioneering a new church in Manchester. Pastor John asked me to come along side him as his co-pastor. It was to be a joint ministry. I was told I had a Pastor's heart and so my ministry began. The Church was called 'Freshfields', and working with Pastor John was a brilliant and enlightening experience. God blessed the work mightily. Many hurting people were saved and healed. We began to grow as a fellowship. (A few years later Pastor John was called to pioneer a church for Messianic Jews called 'Jacobs Ladder'. This too was to become a mighty work and calling.)

One day a young man, Andrew Proctor, came to Freshfields and gave his life to the Lord. He was a singer/songwriter in the secular music world, but after his conversion he said that he'd only sing for God. His life and his music changed so much. One day he asked me to come to his studio to listen to a new song that he'd written. It was beautiful. As I prayed with him for his ministry I felt God telling me to join up with him. He felt it was right too and so and we formed a music ministry team called Opus Music Ministries. Andrew was the lead singer. He wrote, produced and recorded all his own music. In meetings I would give my testimony and preach, and Andrew would minister in song. The blessings were wonderful. In the five years that we ministered together as Opus we saw many people come to the Lord, many being healed and baptized, and we ministered at over two hundred churches. These were exciting times.

Out of all these churches one particular church stands out in my memories. It was an 'open barn' church in a village called Settle. This church was different from all the rest. While the two people in charge were in their fifties, the whole congregation consisted of young people aged between fifteen and twenty two years, who had either Down's syndrome or autism. While we were setting up our sound equipment they started to wander in. These young people had a very childlike innocence. Andrew and I found them to be really loving, friendly and excitable. I'd been very surprised to see them all. Having never ministered to people like these before, I wasn't too certain how to go about it, but I was assured that these children really did love the Lord and would be able to follow everything that was going on. I prayed that the Lord would show me how to reach them so I could speak to them on their own level of understanding, while at the same time not appearing to be condescending. It was a fantastic night and the experience taught me so much. I learned how much love God had for these people just the way they were. They knew all about Jesus, his love, and love for one another and at the end of the meeting they prayed with us. My eyes had been opened.

Our singer, Andrew, just grew and grew as a Christian and was so excited at how God had blessed his ministry. For such a young Christian he had come on in leaps and bounds.

One of our concerts was in a small Church of England in Wrexham, South Wales. Only two people showed up, one being the vicar and the other a lady who was passing by. The beauty of it was that we performed as though we were in front of a full church and the lady got saved. Nothing we gave to God was ever wasted. God used whatever was available.

Occasionally things went more slowly, depending on how much each particular church had prepared itself. Opus Music had its critics too but we both said, "If God be for us who can be against us." This criticism was mostly from more traditional ministers who didn't understand how God would use an ex-convict/ex-tramp and a new Christian in this way.

In the world there are many kinds of people, just as there are many different religions. The Bible teaches us of the Saviour of the world, Jesus Christ and of God's love. Here there is no contradiction, only truth. In the world people are seeking truth, life and its meaning whilst being surrounded by deceit, false hope and false promises. This too was my experience. I'd tried all kinds of 'fulfilment', in order to discover the answer to my emptiness. I'd been a criminal, been chased and wanted by the police, served several years in prison, and played the big tough guy. In prison I'd felt fear from other prisoners as well as from the prison officers. (Consider all the beatings I'd received). After experiencing all this I'd dropped out of society and become a tramp, living on scraps, begging and feeling the awful bitter cold. I became an alcoholic, was shunned by my own family, then when I could sink no lower and must surely have been close to death, I was by 'chance' taken in by a wonderful Christian family, who took the risk of having this stranger living in their home. It was then that I found the answer. I took Jesus as my Saviour and my life was totally transformed. He worked miracles in my life. I saw how God could look down on a person like me and bless me with his salvation. I am saved by His grace. It's His undeserved love and favour for me, as I've not, nor ever could do, anything to deserve it. Thankfully, salvation is founded on what He has done for me, not what I've done for Him.

No matter who you are or what you are, in God's eyes you are special. To that emptiness, to whatever is missing; that reason why we are the way we are, Jesus is the answer. All that you need is Jesus. That cross where he was crucified says it all. When Jesus said on the cross, "It is finished", (John 19 v 30), sin was finished and we have the new beginning. The Bible says, 'I've come that you might have life and life abundantly (in all its fullness) '. (John 10 v 10) The shadow of the cross is the sign that somebody loves us, and that somebody is God. As the scripture says, 'For God so loved the world that He gave is only begotten Son, that whosoever believes in Him shall not perish but have everlasting life.' (John 3:16) The emergency service for our sin, our hurts, and our pain is found in the Bible under the name Jesus.

The spirit of man can be torn away by the tragedies of life. Bitterness is easily consumed and personalities easily destroyed by cruelties. Life can be fair or unfair. There can be rich, lonely people as well as poor, lonely people and sometimes whichever way we turn a closed door awaits. We only have to read the newspapers or watch the television to see the unrest in the world or indeed in our own lives, but life is not a joke, it's real. Every television soap we watch supposedly reflects life in today's society. What a tragedy if this were the truth, if 'soapland' was a true reflection of everyday life. I've been able to see why people drop out of society, and can remember reading headlines referring to the '*Big Black Hope*' or the '*Great White Hope*'—all ending in no hope at all.

Many of my life experiences could so easily have ended in tragedy, but I do have a hope. There is grace and love and peace. There is real life. If we are to point a finger then let us point to the source of all truth, Jesus Christ. Once again here the Bible gives us a clear and positive truth.

Jesus said, "I am the Way, the Truth and the Life..." (John 14:6) The Way is to be challenged and proven. In my experience I've found it proven. I couldn't have written this book if it weren't so. In desperation I wanted to end my life, but in Christ I found new life. I've been fulfilled.

There is a great work to be done out there in this world. There are people out there now who are very similar to me when I was on the street, or a criminal, or in prison. These people need to be found and shown God's love and compassion.

I've quoted the words from a song written by a friend that encapsulates what I am saying:

You'll find me on the corner of a street in every town,

In the hooded youth who's searching for life's meaning.

You'll find me in the playground, by the swings and all around,

In the lonely teenage mother who's waiting to be found.

When you helped the very least,

The least of all my children. When you helped the very least

You have fed and clothed ... and ministered to me.

You'll find me on a park bench,   and walking through the city,

In the homeless and the hopeless, looking for a meal.

You'll find me in back alleys, where the winos clutch their drinks,

And the junkie sits there shaking, craving his next fix.

When you helped the very least,

The least of all my children. When you helped the very least

Then You fed and clothed ... and ministered to me.   ©

Likewise there is also a need for the Gospel to be preached amongst the rich and famous. The tabloids show us that pop groups and film stars, even with all their wealth are still searching for fulfilment. This fulfilment can be found. Material wealth comes to an end but spiritual wealth is eternal. It's easy; it's priceless. It's found at the cross and it can be your beginning.

I am now in the position where I've given my testimony in many places to numerous people, but all the praise goes to God to whom I am so thankful. He gave me my salvation, a marvellous new beginning, a new start. On many occasions I've been asked why I haven't written a book about my life, but until recently I'd not felt the Lord's prompting to do so. My life so far has consisted of a variety of happenings, some foolish but most very good. I've seen many people come to the Lord and have spoken to many who have been in situations similar to my own.

I would like to thank all the people who have positively influenced my life, especially my new family, who just obeyed God's word to love and pray for me. I am also eternally grateful to God, who led me to so many good Pastors who showed me so much understanding. The Lord has used me to reach out, counsel and love people in such hard situations.

Whilst I was going through a particularly bad phase I had the good fortune to meet Chris and Amanda Proctor. They cared, and prayed for me and kept their home open to me at a time when I really needed good friends. This is what belonging to a family is all about. Many, many people become Christians and we are all one family, but this family's individual members still have problems and needs. We should always be there for each other, helping one another so that no one gets left behind. After all, Jesus is always there for us, in the hard times and the good times, and as believers we are supposed to model our lives after His.

I am waiting for the second coming, the Lord's return, when the Bible says, 'I shall see my Saviour face to face'. I and countless others will see His glory and say, "Thank you Lord". Then I'll see my name in the Lamb's Book of Life.

You do not have to be a tramp or a criminal, or to have been in prison to know Jesus, but if you are lost and in despair remember that Jesus is the answer.

'I pray that God will bless and anoint this book, using it to reach others, and that you the reader will find out how great our God really is. Amen.'

18.

Your Next Step

You are valuable to God, no matter how low you think you have gone, or how little value you place upon yourself, and no matter what you have done, or if you consider yourself an ordinary person who has lead a 'good' life, you matter to God. He loves you and He sent His son, Jesus, to die in your place. The Lord of all creation considers you worth dying for! That is the enormous value He places upon you. Jesus Christ, The creator of the universe was willing to die in your place, and He did.

Romans 5:7 tells us, 'We can understand someone dying for a person worth dying for, and we can understand how someone good and noble could inspire us to selfless sacrifice. But God put his love on the line for us by offering his Son in sacrificial death while we were of no use whatever to him.'

If the message in this book has touched you in any way, and you would like to experience what I experienced through the saving grace of God, the following is a prayer you might like to use to lead you to salvation and the great love that God has for you.

'Lord Jesus I never realised why you died for me and how much you loved me and suffered on that cross so that I might have life. I am truly sorry and repent of all my wrong doings and I ask you now Lord Jesus to come into my life. Please cleanse me of sin, wash me and fill me with that love. Please write my name in The Lamb's Book of Life, and may I experience the wonderful love of God in my life.

I thank you for coming into my life and making me a child of the living God. I now receive and accept Jesus as my personal Saviour and believe that I am now Born Again, a Christian, a new child in Christ. Amen.'

If you prayed this prayer, and meant it, you are Born Again. You need to speak to God and read his word, the Bible, every day. This is how you build a relationship with Him. You may never have prayed before but it's quite easy really, you just speak to him as you would to a friend. You should also find yourself a good Bible believing, Christian church where you can go and get to know other believers who will help and encourage you.

I would love to hear from you too.

You can contact me at: tramps47@yahoo.co.uk

God has a plan for your life. The Bible says in Jeremiah 29:11 'For I know the plans I have for you declares the Lord, plans to prosper you and not to harm you, plans to give you hope and a future.' He helped and guided me and he will do the same for you.

Some readers will have been believers for some time. I would like to encourage you in that no matter what you do for God, whether in your thinking it's small or great, nothing is ever wasted. Even if no one else notices, God will. You may think that because of age or infirmity you can do nothing but pray, but this is a wonderful ministry. God will use it for His glory in the furtherance of His kingdom. All we have to do is to be obedient to Him. We may never know what a difference we have made.

19.

P.S.

The Bible tells us in Isaiah 58:7 -

'I want you to share your food with the hungry and bring right into your own homes those who are helpless, poor and destitute. Clothe those who are cold and do not hide from relatives who need your help'.

This is just what that kind lady and her family did for me. It was a huge sacrifice for the whole family to take in a destitute person, but through their obedience my life was changed beyond belief. I became a Christian and God used, and still uses me to reach others, so He can touch them and work in their lives. These people in turn will also have reached many others. So you see what you do for God has a ripple effect, like dropping a small pebble in a pond.

Be encouraged, the following verse (Isaiah 58:8) tells us of the blessings that will follow the instruction in verse 7.

'Then shall your light break forth like the morning, and your healing (your restoration and the power of a new life) shall spring forth speedily; your righteousness, (your rightness, your justice, and your right relationship with God) shall go before you conducting you to peace and prosperity, and the glory of the Lord shall be your rear guard.'

I'm glad I have been able to write this story; I am glad my eyes have been opened. Life's questions can be answered, and doors of opportunity can open. I cannot say that I am happy with all I went through in my life, but it proved to me that everyone can be given new life.

May God bless you in your walk with Him. Amen.

* * *

- Pastor Les Deane is now the manager of Freshfields Christian Music Ministries and is available to speak at meetings.

He and can be contacted at tramps47@yahoo.co.uk